Nights of Hunger

A Cocktail of Grief, Dreams & Dating for
Old-Ass Women

Pamela Katims Steele, PhD

Book Cover art by Matt Grosvold and design by Michelle Steele

1st edition 2025

Contents

bless the thing

that broke you down

and cracked you

open

because the world

needs you open

—Rebecca Campbell

From *The Fellowship of the River* by Joseph Tafur, MD

Prologue

On August 10, 2020, tragedy struck, turning my world upside down. On the edge of an empty parking lot in the back of an inn on the Oregon coast, my husband, Patrick, fell down to the ground, smashing his head on the concrete. My phone was in the car. The parking lot was empty. I was horrified, vacillating between different, desperate options: 911 or CPR? Or should I yell for help? The rooms at the inn faced west toward the ocean, not east toward the parking lot, so getting someone's attention was difficult. Shocked, I discovered I had no cell service. My efforts to reach 911 were in vain.

Patrick and I had only been at the inn for four hours. It was the beginning of what was to be a three-night stay to celebrate our thirty-ninth anniversary. When we arrived, Patrick said he was tired and wanted to rest, which seemed reasonable, given that he had driven for nearly six hours. I walked to the beach by myself to check out the ease of the access point, considering Patrick's bad knee. When I returned, he said he was cold. That also seemed logical, as all three windows were open; I also felt it was chilly.

I lay down on the bed next to him, watching the news. Every few minutes I asked him how he felt. He wasn't feeling "right." Over the years, he had had four cardioversions and two ablations for AFIB, so I immediately thought *heart problems*. While he was adamant, saying no, it wasn't his heart but rather his lungs, he was soon saying he wanted to go home.

We packed up our things and headed for the car, never telling anyone we were leaving. Besides, it was early COVID, and there was no one to tell. Patrick knew we were in for a drive of about four to five hours, and I knew that we would pass by the closest hospital on our way.

The car was loaded, and we were standing at the open trunk when he looked at me and said, "Oh no."

Then, he fell.

Ultimately, another guest came to my aid. He continued CPR while I tried reaching 911 on his phone and was thankfully able to share our location before the line went dead. Soon, the medics, police, and firefighters arrived, worked on my love, and loaded him into the medic van. A police officer said I could follow him in our car, but since my fingers and toes were tingling, I said, "No, not a good idea." He agreed to give me a ride.

When we arrived at the hospital, I asked the officer to find a wheelchair for me, afraid that if I stood up, I would faint. I knew I needed to be "present" for my husband—not be another patient.

Due to COVID precautions, I was told to sit in the hospital waiting room. When I was finally allowed into the treatment room, I found Patrick attached to multiple machines. The doctor came to my side, softly reporting that her team could not find a pulse.

All the 'what if' scenarios Patrick and I had discussed over the years raced through my head. No heroics. Quality of life is more important than quantity. I knew what I had to do. "You have to let him go," I said in a daze. A simple, though not easy, decision.

The doctor looked shocked when I made that declaration so quickly. They kept trying to get a pulse but I knew his brain had been without oxygen for too long. I guessed thirty minutes. Later, I learned it had been twenty-six.

Patrick's death was not my first experience dealing with a major loss. But it was by far the most traumatic.

My parents and only sibling died between 2006 and 2008. Yes, all of them. I was forced to learn a tremendous amount about death, dying, and grief in a hurry. At the time, I was working in a trauma hospital and was incredibly fortunate to have access to any physician and other much-needed resources. Thankfully, my husband was alive then and supported me through the grieving process and all the administrivia that follows a death (or several, like in my case).

Subsequent to retiring from the hospital, and after my own near-death experience resulted in an emergency hysterectomy, I decided to focus on helping others understand more about death, dying, the relevant medical terminology, and the importance of creating a clear and specific advance healthcare directive. I taught classes. I made presentations. I consulted with individual families—all because I was determined to help ease the pain and suffering of other survivors. While being prepared is a gift for the one who is dying, it is especially so for those left behind to do the clean-up while they're grieving.

That brings us back to 2020. Patrick died at my feet, literally. I had no 911 connection. As I looked at his body, my mind flew in multiple directions. I realized I knew nothing . . . *nothing* about traumatic loss. All the people I had worked with to date had relatives who were on a steady decline. They had time for goodbyes, laughter, and tears. They had time to pass on critical knowledge. Time to share memories.

I had nothing. No time. No words. And I was alone with my loss for the first twenty-two hours.

1

Surviving in the Pit of Darkness

Fifteen days after Patrick died, I had a powerful and prescient dream. I dreamed I woke up in a hospital, only to discover that my left arm had been amputated. I looked at the doctor—someone with whom I had attended high school—in absolute horror, in shock. His comment? "Oops, I made a mistake. Sue me." My mouth remained agape in horror and disbelief.

"No, I really didn't," he said next. "It wasn't going to make it anyway."

In the dream, I remember thinking, *It's my left arm, not my right. I am severely injured and will never be the same. But I am not totally incapacitated.*

For me, this was an empowering dream. It helped me realize that, as empty and lost as I felt, I could find my way through the morass. I could slog through the unknown with the full awareness that it would require a tremendous amount of patience and grace. My Type A personality was not going to be my friend.

Thinking of that time, I am reminded of the Buddhist phrase, "No mud, no lotus." In very basic terms, it means we have to wade through the muck before we can blossom and grow. Running away from pain and suffering, distracting ourselves with food, drink, television, and more, only delays the healing process.

There is value in learning how to embrace the pain and calm it down. There is value in accepting the messiness of life. There is value in seeing the struggle as nourishment. Only then can we emerge from underwater and begin to recognize and appreciate beauty, happiness, and growth.

When our life is filled with joy, we're busy relishing its bounty. But it is through change, suffering, and challenge that we grow and become stronger.

In spite of that optimistic sense of empowerment, I spent close to three years feeling neutralized and numb, unable to feel or express any emotion other than bewilderment. I contemplated leaving this earthly plane, but I couldn't do that to my kids. They, too, were experiencing trauma, though in a very different way. Their lives were naturally busy, so moving on was easier. Me? I was just left with my own thoughts, my own pain, and my rather wobbly determination to survive, with little knowledge of how to do so.

People always say that the shortest distance between points A and B is a straight line. Few journeys in life are like that. Truthfully, sometimes I can't even define point B, let alone figure out how to get there. And as you've no doubt heard, if you don't know where you're going, any road will get you there.

There are many lessons in trusting the process and letting go of that fruitless temptation to control the uncontrollable. In realizing that there are worthwhile hints, helpers, and messages that deserve to be listened to. Doing new things and meeting new people seemed worth my time and energy.

It took me close to three years to even entertain the idea of dating and potentially finding a trustworthy companion. Perhaps someone else could help bring light and joy back into my life.

After spending over half my life married to an exceptional human being, I'll admit that the world of dating seemed like navigating a jungle in a foreign land where even charades fail as a form of communication.

As I thought about writing a book, it seemed only appropriate to weave a story about the intersection of grief, dreams, new identities, and new loves. This is now my life, and all these aspects feed into who I am and who I'm becoming.

2
A Map to the Maze of My Mind

Time is ephemeral. Sometimes it stands still. Sometimes its speed is overwhelming. Sometimes it's just a meaningless meander.

As I take you on my journey, you'll need to forget about the concept of time as you know it. Because my stories won't be linear.

Three months into my grieving, I decided to set up a challenge. The goal was to extract myself from the emotional quicksand, nudge myself forward, and prevent catatonia—or risk becoming one with my bed.

The challenge was to use Patrick's death as a discovery process, perhaps an adventure, rather than a "sentence." I asked myself how I could use my pain to learn and grow. How could I move from victim mode to empowered mode? What positives could possibly emerge from his death?

I decided to ask myself a different question every day and make note of my responses in a journal. In retrospect, I adopted the "fake it till you make it" mentality, believing that I certainly couldn't make my situation any worse. Admittedly, I was quite reluctant to commit to this exercise, but as a determined and sometimes stubborn individual, I pushed on. Needless to say, some questions and some days were tougher than others. But I persevered. Now, five years later, I'm able to look back and champion my progress.

Will I ever be without the pain of loss? No! As I have shared with a spousal loss grief group, of which I am one of several facilitators, that pain will always be there, but the amount of space it occupies in my heart will grow smaller over time as my world expands.

It was around mid-2023 when I decided to enter the world of online dating. What follows here is a combination of my thirty-day journaling exercise, my online dating adventures (the men's names have been changed, of course), the relevance and importance of dreams, and what I've learned as I continue to travel this road.

3

An Invitation to a Nudist Camp

My very first date with someone I met on an online dating site was for happy hour at a local restaurant that was easily reachable for both of us. We arrived at the same time, and I quickly found myself enveloped in a hug. Grant was tall, clean shaven, and well dressed in casual slacks, a nice shirt, and a jacket for warmth.

Once seated at an outdoor table, I ordered a drink. He did not. I don't recall feeling nervous. I'm a self-confident person who figured I had nothing to lose. *Put yourself out there and see what happens*, I had told myself. No one was holding a gun to my head, and I was always free to walk away.

Grant's most recent long-term partner had died. I don't recall how long ago. He had been her caretaker until the end. I understood she was considerably older than him, but they'd had a lot of shared interests. At that time, he was clearly trying to figure out his next steps, including whether or not he should keep his condo on the east side of the lake. It seemed like he was in limbo, waiting to see if he could find his next mate before he made a decision.

Our conversation was wide-ranging, flowed naturally, and included stories about travel adventures, certainly one of my interests. Seemingly out of nowhere, Grant invited me to go to a nudist retreat center in southern France. His treat. Evidently, he and his now-deceased partner had enjoyed a variety of nudist adventures during their years together. I'd never been invited to a nudist retreat anywhere, let alone in France. Suffice it to say, I laughed and politely declined his offer.

As we were saying our goodbyes, he invited me to a local annual fair the following week. I agreed to join him. Happy hour had been pleasant enough, so I was open to learning more about him. I didn't want to jump to an unwarranted conclusion. I needed more data before making any decisions.

It was raining on the day of the fair, so we went to a movie instead and then out to dinner. He paid, by the way, though I did offer to split the check.

I had taken a now half-empty water bottle from the movie with me to the restaurant. Tossing it away had seemed wasteful. It was a casual restaurant and an easy walk from the theater. We sat in the bar and I placed my bottle on the small table in front of me. "Really? I thought you had some class." He said these words quite casually.

I was rather taken aback. Was that a joke? Sarcasm? I'll never know.

After dinner, he walked me back to my condo, his arm around me. I admit—it felt good but not *that* good. When he asked about seeing me again, I replied that I had enjoyed his company but if he was looking for something more meaningful, I was not the one.

In all fairness, perhaps I jumped the gun. Perhaps I should have said, "Let's continue to learn more about each other." But his values were clear to me, and after only two meetings, I knew I didn't share them.

And so ended attempt one.

Later that week, I started my journaling saga. Here's how that went.

JOURNALING DAY 1

How are you feeling right now and how does that compare to how you felt when you were with Patrick?

The emptiness in my life is palpable. I don't know who I am anymore. I don't know what to do.

Loss rearranges your sense of self. You are no longer the person you were. That person is gone.

It's like someone came in while you were asleep and rearranged everything inside. All familiar things are lost, though the outside remains the same. You are not what or who you once were.

And while life is always a series of personal reinventions, this time—this time—feels different.

I used to be part of an amazing couple. So joyful, so optimistic, sometimes even "accused" of being a Pollyanna—and at other times of being the Energizer Bunny. Someone who wanted to get up in the morning to embrace the day, always ready for the next adventure. I used to talk more, laugh more, eat more. I cried less and slept less.

I used to spend *way* more time supporting other people rather than being immersed in my own pain or problems.

I never shrank from a challenge, as I knew, after forty years of navigating life together with Patrick, that we could accomplish anything.

Knowing his gifts as well as I did, I knew I could always rely on him to explore new ideas with me, devise creative approaches to problems, and flat-out handle things that were foreign to me. I used to depend on him to be there . . . for joy, love, hugs, and life.

4
My Online Persona

Notes: Once I decided to enter the online dating world, I had to create a profile.

I've had inquiries from all over the country, even though my profile clearly states, "Near Seattle, please." All the photos I include in my profile are recent and reflective of several of my interests. Not so true of many others who are on the hunt. If the men online choose to read instead of just looking at pictures (as shown below), this is what they'll learn about me.

"Near Seattle, please! I am a friendly, outgoing person who believes in open, honest, and authentic communication. Check out my photos to see that I'm ready for a variety of adventures. I'm intellectually savvy, exercise lots of common sense, and have a warm, kind heart. I am a staunch believer in lifelong learning, am open to new ideas, and love to travel and read.

"For fun, give me a racquet or a paddle and I'm a happy camper—tennis, pickleball, ping-pong, you name it. Yes, exercise is important to me. If it's in the sunshine, even better. Love to bury my toes in the sand on a beach, especially an ocean beach.

"Give me a soapbox and I'll talk about racial and gender equity, abortion rights, criminal justice reform, and equal access to quality and affordable healthcare (including mental healthcare) and education (including preschool).

"I am passionate, sometimes intense, competitive, organized, tenacious, and empathetic. It's fair to say I have high standards—for myself and others.

"Contributing to a greater good and making a difference in my community is important to me. Whether answering calls at the crisis clinic, facilitating a spousal loss grief group, or chairing a scholarship committee, I'm all about listening and encouraging others to be their best self.

"You can probably tell I'm quite comfortable in my own skin. I'm great being on my own but also love being part of a team.

"Sports, adventure, theater, movies, great music, art, good food and wine? I'm in!"

About me:
Relationship: Widow / Widower
Have kids: Yes, and they live away from home
Want kids: No
Education: Graduate degree, PhD
Body type: Athletic/Fit
Height: 5'5" (165 cm)
Faith: Spiritual but not religious
Smoke: No
Drink: In moderation, of course

JOURNALING DAY 2

How would I like people to approach me in my current state of grieving? What do I want them to know?

Don't make assumptions. Your eyes and my words might fool you. All my life, I've heard about how strong I am, how independent. Even my husband would sometimes say, "Don't you ever *need* anybody?"

As I was growing up, my parents used to say, "Remember who you are." That was another way of saying, "Keep it together, be good, people know who you are and your behavior will reflect on us." So you bet—I know how to put a good face on anything . . . almost.

But the loss of my soulmate has brought me to my knees. I'm in free fall, no solid ground to stand on, crossing a chasm to a new, as yet unexplored, undefined land. This will be a long journey, an endless transformation. I know that.

What I need are some loving, brave companions who will be patient, quietly appreciative, and quietly aware that we'll all grow and learn together, one step at a time. Don't let me fool you. Please.

Messages and signals keep telling me I'm able to handle all this shock and trauma. Yet, in one of my early dreams, I found myself in the midst of extreme chaos and confusion—I had discovered that all my money, credit cards, and ID were stolen. After slowing down and concentrating on a search, I managed to locate my cash but nothing else. I carefully reviewed everything I thought I had lost and admitted that I needed to deal with my reality one step at a time. And perhaps I can be smart enough to admit that I might not be able to handle everything on my own. Clearly my dream was telling me that my ability to juggle effectively was not as good as I had imagined. I needed to prioritize and differentiate between the important and the urgent.

5
Dog Walker, Too

I gotta say that Charles had a great sense of humor in his online communication. His tantalizing and engaging text messages had me laughing or at least smiling. When I met him face to face, he was wearing a T-shirt that read, "The End of an Error." The T-shirt was from January 2021. Clearly, he and I agreed politically. That's important to me.

At the time, Charles was dealing with a knee injury and was unable to give his dog a good walk. Dog lover and compassionate person that I am, I volunteered to come to his house, which was fairly close, and walk the dog. Seemed like a helpful and very low-risk way to meet someone. The humans were clearly more excited about this prospect than the pooch. He did all he could to force me to turn around and take him home.

After the walk, Charles invited me in for homemade banana bread and coffee. As I looked around the living area and used the bathroom, it was clear to me that the house was neglected and needed repairs and renovations. Things looked ragged. Was he a single man with no taste or perhaps no money? Then again, perhaps home repair and upkeep were low-priority tasks to him.

Perhaps he just didn't care. Some might call me picky, but I don't like clutter, nor am I comfortable in a mess. To me, how a man takes care of himself and his surroundings says a lot. A former colleague of mine used to say, "Cluttered room, cluttered mind." I think there's some truth to that.

As we sat in the eating area in his cramped kitchen, we talked about our backgrounds and our work. Interestingly, Charles and I had both completed our graduate studies at the same university and had even taken a number of courses from the same professors. On paper, we had a lot in common. But, once more, I felt rather blasé about the interaction and lack of chemistry. I had no desire to pursue a relationship with this man, either.

JOURNALING DAY 3

How do my surroundings feel given that I'm living in the space I once shared with Patrick? Would I rather be elsewhere?

I can live anywhere. The desert, the forest, the beach, the mountains. There is beauty in every landscape. Sure, I have favorites. But given enough time, enough patience, and enough mindfulness, I can learn to appreciate my surroundings.

But no one told me what I'd find in this altered landscape. Honestly, I had no warning that there would even *be* an altered landscape. One minute, I was living in heaven. The next minute,

I found myself in hell. In a split second, life as I knew it changed forever. And now, here's a forced "opportunity" to live in a new reality, a new landscape, one that is invisible to others, one they can't begin to comprehend. I can't comprehend it either. I'm still struggling to understand it. Still struggling to accept it.

The spotlight is now on my *internal* landscape. You know, that vapid one that feels so cold, whose organizing principle is a starvation of the heart. Living in that landscape is the issue. Living with that feeling of being alone. Not lonely. *Alone.* With the constant refrain, "Wherever you go, there you are."

So how do I learn to live in this new landscape? I'll start by admitting that I don't know the answer to that question. Not yet.

What I *do* know is that our old mantra (Patrick's and mine) of "Just get 'er done, dude," won't work now. My Type A approach won't work now. I'm on a roller coaster, and I'm blindfolded. I don't know where the next twist and turn will be; I don't know when I'll face a steep climb or when I'll drop into an abyss. I'm strapped in. There's no escaping. I can't get my money back. I hate this ride!

Obviously, this requires a new playbook. I refuse to play the victim. The best I can do right now is to be patient with myself, become my own caregiver, and hold myself with compassion and patience. Not my normal MO. In the words of Baba Ram Dass (yes, I'm a child of the sixties), "Be Here Now."

Note: So strange that last night, I heard Patrick's voice through the ether: "I did not want to do that. I wasn't ready to go."

6
Some Messages Are Clear

E arly on, dreams beset me almost every night. Some I was able to recall as complete stories. Others were so fragmented that I found them impossible to capture. Some nights I wonder if I've really slept, even now. My mind is so busy or so it seems. My dream-movies unfurl in a never-ending stream:

1) There are huge water leaks coming through the ceiling fixtures, all of them. Nobody seems to care; no one knows what to do. I'm surrounded by an uncontrollable mess.

2) I'm driving along a beach road that just ends. A woman stands in front of my car, forcing me to quickly slow down. As she walks toward my car, she begs to be killed.

3) There is a symphony of calming "whoosh" noises in my head. I am surrounded by perfectly balanced, comforting sounds. Then a visual is added: Leaves gently fly in from both sides of my body, coming together in a soft but straight line, like a guiding path.

4) I force my right foot into a shoe that is way too small for me. Patrick comments on how nice it looks, saying, "That's the size I really always imagined your foot to be."

To me, the first three dreams represent the chaotic nature of each day following Patrick's death. Everything was a mess. Could I handle this rock 'n' roll ride? Could I figure out how to put one foot in front of the other, keep breathing, and tackle the necessary tasks? Did I even want to? Then came the self-talk: *Slow down, be patient, give yourself some grace.*

The fourth dream? That one required more introspection, asking myself some tough questions. Did I force myself to be smaller in our life together than I was authentically? Was my extrovert personality sometimes too much for my more introverted husband? Was I too achievement-oriented for him? Did I hold myself back, assuming that he would be uncomfortable with my choices? Did I make assumptions rather than have discussions?

Unfortunately, I think I did. I would definitely handle our time together differently if I had a chance for a repeat performance.

7
Friends with Benefits

During one of my visits with a healthcare provider, she asked if I would be open to meeting another client of hers, someone she thought might be a good match. I agreed. After all, why not? Meeting someone through a mutual friend has a much higher probability of success than meeting a complete unknown from a dating site.

She described him as a very bright man, financially stable, creative, travel loving, nice looking, etc. We were both widowed, though his wife had passed several years prior after a long illness. In addition, he had lost another family member in a traumatic accident, so he was very familiar with both types of loss, anticipatory and traumatic. He would understand the anguish I was experiencing.

Jake and I had several lengthy phone conversations, all of which were quite interesting. I would characterize them as more academic in nature as I was fascinated by his scientific, medically related work.

On our first date, he took me out to dinner. The rain was coming down in torrents. Not unusual in Seattle. When he picked me up, I quickly jumped into the car, saying, "Hi!" as if we were old friends. Somehow, it felt like that after our lengthy phone calls.

The car didn't move. We just sat there as he stared at me. That was uncomfortable. I squirm when someone stares at me and says nothing. My guess is that he had ideas of what I looked like, and they didn't match the reality.

For his part, Jake had a beautiful head of white hair and was neatly dressed in a pair of khaki pants, a good-looking shirt, and sweater.

Our dinner conversation, much of it health- and research-related, was interesting. During the meal, I also learned that he was taking tennis lessons at a beautiful private club and enjoyed playing pickleball. These were activities that we could share.

By the end of the evening, it seemed reasonable to meet again and continue to learn about each other.

I invited Jake to my place for dinner a week or so later. While I was prepping the food before his arrival, I received a text from him with a link, asking me to complete a quiz to determine my love language. This, he believed, would help us better understand each other and communicate more effectively.

First off, I didn't have time for that. I'm a busy person. Number two, for me, that was rushing things. "I don't even know if I really like you," I muttered to myself, "so please hold off on this idea."

As we ate our dinner, he asked me if I liked waterbeds. That question came out of nowhere and again seemed quite premature. *You're asking me that on a second date?* I thought incredulously.

In spite of my mixed emotions, I agreed to another date, a dinner at his house, another place I wanted to remodel and redecorate. Of course, that thought remained silently embedded in my mind. I didn't say a thing. We ate our dinner in a tiny cubby hole of an eating space in the kitchen, even though there was a lovely dining room.

The conversation—rather, *his* conversation—turned to sex. He started telling me about dreams he'd had about his wife and their love-making. Frankly, I didn't care. As I could plainly see where this conversation was headed, I told him straight out that I was not ready for an intimate relationship with anyone—at which point he suggested that friends with benefits was an acceptable alternative.

"No, not with me," was my answer.

I laugh while writing what happened next: He asked me about all the other widows in my building. Hard pass.

I put on my big puffy coat (I so appreciated the bodily protection in that moment), thanked him for dinner, hugged him goodbye, and left.

JOURNALING DAY 4

Can I still smell Patrick—in the few items of his clothing I still have or in our bed?

After three broken noses, all sports-related, Patrick and I used to joke about my nose. He'd say it was on my face just so I'd look like a normal human being. If I peeled off the mask that is my face, there would be no nose. It was all part of our jokes about both of us being from other planets. This one had way too much water for Patrick. We were definitely from different planets, raised on distinctly different sides of the tracks. The odds of our meeting were not good. But not only did we meet; we also recognized each other from our former lives. Our connection was deep and historic. We had always been entwined.

Patrick was a clean freak. I, the neat freak. His body was clean. His clothes were clean. And he never wore aftershave, as all perfume scents gave him a headache. I regretted that one, as I liked to nuzzle into his neck and smell some aftershave. That was early on in our relationship, before he started having the headache reaction. Too bad, as the smell of aftershave always excited me.

8
Discoveries on the Road

A s I've been on this journey for the last four years, I've learned a lot of things about myself and the dating world:

1. Once I determine that there might be a connection with someone, I prefer to meet them face-to-face as early as possible. Simply texting back and forth can be very misleading. I've learned this the hard way more than once. Some of these so-called eligible bachelors are nothing more than aspiring scam artists. With others, after meeting in person, I simply had no interest. Early on in multiple text exchanges, I've been asked to provide my phone number or email address. While that does make communication a lot easier and faster, that's a "hard no" until we've met and I see how I feel.

2. I have my own personal litmus test. Can I imagine even kissing you? For most men thus far, the answer has been no. Given that, I truly wonder if I am even capable of feeling any sexual energy with another man. Have I become the walking dead?

3. In relation to sexual energy, it's probably appropriate to share that I had an emergency and total hysterectomy in 2006. My right ovary had made two complete rotations and was necrotic, resulting in 25 to 30 percent of my body's blood collecting in my abdomen. It nearly killed me. I'm thankful that I listened to my body and got back to the hospital that had discharged me hours earlier. The silver lining here is that the doctors discovered borderline ovarian cancer. Ovarian cancer killed Patrick's mother at the age of forty-seven, so you can well imagine his state of mind as he sat alone in the waiting room during my five-hour surgery.

Between my age, non-existent sex organs, and Patrick's death, perhaps you can understand my uncertainty around my ability to ever feel aroused again.

I'm happy to report that between the wonders of estradiol and testosterone and my introduction to "The Northerner" (see Chapter 13), I'm quasi-functional when it comes to sex. I say "quasi" because I still have some post-surgical challenges.

JOURNALING DAY 5

Do I have a companion on this journey? If so, who?

I'd introduce myself, but it seems we've met. I'm grief.

But really, I'm not that simple. I'm a hybrid. A mixture of grief, trauma, and shock. You'll get to know me better in time. Actually, you'll learn to live with me . . . eventually.

I know - you didn't ask for a new companion. And certainly not me. But I'm here now. That shadow of inexplicable weight. A shadow that continually morphs and catches you off-guard, the one that sits beside you on that roller-coaster ride you've talked about. I can squeeze into the smallest, most awkward places. I can appear at the most inopportune time. I'm basically unpredictable, amorphous, omnipresent. I'm that ache in your heart, that knot in your gut, the cotton ball stuck in your throat, cutting off your air. I'm lodged in your brain, clouding your thinking and garbling your words. I'm sorry. I know this isn't comforting.

You won't believe this now but I'm not all bad. I actually have some lessons to teach. Yes, they're painful and quite challenging. But you've always described yourself as a lifelong learner. Right?

Okay, okay . . . so you're not ready to hear that now. No doubt, in your eyes, I'm not much more than a sumo wrestler trying to take you down.

I'll be whatever you need me to be. But I will *be*. I will be here, in some form, *forever*.

9

Hope Meets Reality

Part A

I exchanged several rounds of texts with Sam, a man who seemed to be a perfect match for me. He was a psychologist from a neighborhood just north of mine. It seemed we had so much in common that I was truly looking forward to meeting him. *OMG*, I exclaimed mentally, *this will be perfect; it will be great.*

Sam was a divorcee and had two daughters. He lived on one side of a duplex with his ex-wife on the other, an arrangement that allowed the girls to visit both parents easily.

Our coffee date generated a very different OMG reaction. The conversation was anything but easy. It was work -- hard work. It's natural to draft explanations or excuses in your mind when things don't go as planned; you're hard-wired to guess why things feel that way, but it's only speculation, and I'm not sure of its value.

To add to the discomfort, Sam spent most of the hour hacking and coughing into his handkerchief. He shouldn't have even agreed to meet me that day. The circumstances were not conducive to relaxation, his or mine.

Things felt stiff and awkward from the beginning. We stood at the counter, and each ordered coffee and a pastry. When the barista totaled up the bill, we both just stood there for a minute. Sam said nothing and did nothing. Awkward silence. So I just offered my card and paid for all of it. Maybe that was off-putting to him.

Our rendezvous was saved by a car show in the town streets, so after coffee, we wandered around, looked at vintage cars, and were saved by fun conversations with the car owners. A reprieve from awkwardness. So grateful for that car show.

Needless to say, that date ended back at our respective cars. We never contacted each other again.

Part B

Later that afternoon, I met another gentleman for lunch. Yes, it was a busy day.

And what a contrast it was! John's wife had died of brain cancer about three years earlier. Being a nurse, he had cared for her at home. We chatted for several hours over drinks and lunch. The conversation flowed naturally, easily, comfortably. There was an immediate understanding of each other's tenderness and grief. We were willing to be vulnerable with each other because of the level of mutual trust.

John was the first widower I had met. It wasn't until meeting him that I realized how much more at ease I was (and still am) with a widower than with someone who's divorced or who has never been married. Sharing stories, memories, tears, and laughter is all okay. There is no judgment. There are no excuses. There are no comments about needing to let go of the past. What's there is a level of understanding and compassion that is missing from interactions with others.

John and I actually went out five times. Both of us approached the relationship very slowly, very cautiously. One night, while having dinner at my place, I learned that John had some residual complications following prostate cancer. These complications caused him great concern and embarrassment and, though he didn't share it with me at the time, he believed they stood in the way of a healthy relationship.

One day, I visited him at his house, got a tour, and saw his beautiful garden. I was very surprised to see that his wife's bedclothes and hat (from her chemo sessions) still lay on the bed. They were just missing her body. All her things were untouched—in the closets, in the drawers, around the house.

Everyone responds differently to the grief of losing a spouse. Some people clear out their partner's belongings within the first year. Others go a long time before doing so. There are no rights and wrongs.

In the end, John wrote me a letter in which he shared that the chemistry he felt was overpowering, stimulating, and exciting. But being with me was like walking on a knife's edge, as he was always wondering if he could keep things under control. It was a beautiful, loving, vulnerable letter. Several texts later, he made it clear. No more. Too painful to keep up any communication. I honor him for being loyal to himself and his needs.

Months later, I still think about reaching out to see how he's doing.

10
Switchbacks and Reflections

E arly on, my mind was like that of a jackrabbit, flitting from one topic to the next, with no connection between each. Dreams, nightmares, questions, anxiety, guilt, emptiness—all melted together. So much self-questioning, examining, wondering. Welcome to one of those days . . .

Dreams offer us a peek into our subconscious, allowing us to explore unresolved questions or issues. Only the dreamer can make sense of the emotions, thoughts, and symbols that might be reflected in the images.

Snippet One: One month following Patrick's death, I dreamed I grabbed a gun out of a guy's hands. I got him in a chokehold only to discover his neck was scrawny like a bird's.

Message: I tried to save Patrick from himself but he was too weak. I was too late.

Snippet Two: I put all my dollar bills under glass to protect them.

Message: Patrick handled our financial investments. Now what? How in the world do I learn about investments when I am overwhelmed by grief and confusion!?

Snippet Three: I was being carried down the street in a white, satin-lined coffin. Everyone was mourning my death. But . . . I wasn't dead.

Message: I mourn my loss. I mourn the person I no longer am and will never be again.

Snippet Four: A court-appointed social worker came to our house to assess our home environment. Our daughter, who was in her early teens in this dream, was in the family room surrounded by toys and games, in the midst of which was a large rubber penis. The social worker was not impressed. Whose was that? Certainly not mine!

Message: Not sure I know. Will I ever see another penis? Do I care?

Reflections

It's very easy and perhaps only natural to get lost in the "woulda, coulda, shoulda" cycle of self-accusations and guilt-tripping.

My watch died at about 4 p.m. on the day Patrick died. After mentioning it to Patrick, I forgot about it. When he started complaining about not feeling well, why didn't I think about my watch? Was it trying to tell me something? Would I have even recognized the coincidence or thought about it at the time?

Why was he so anxious to leave the art gallery we visited before heading to the inn? Was he already feeling different, unusual, strange?

Why did he keep telling me he was going to be fine? Why did I believe him? Why didn't I call 911 right away? Did he *really* believe he was going to be okay? Why was he so damn stubborn?

Bottom line: *Why, why, why did you leave me? Couldn't you have "played" this differently? Did you have a flash of terror? It all happened so fast! Life feels so empty.*

What is my subconscious telling me? How much of it is driven by guilt? How do I know? Can I really know?

I dreamed that an office in which I worked was to be cleared out immediately and turned into a safe space for sick, elderly people who had nowhere to go. I took what I believed to be all of my belongings and moved to a different part of the building. When I returned to my former office to make sure I hadn't left anything behind, I was stunned to see that the place was already occupied by six or seven old, sickly men in bed, each with a woman sitting by his side.

I heard a voice saying from somewhere, "You get a reprieve."

I walked into an adjoining room where there was still one middle-aged person working. She looked at me and said, "Freedom. That's all there is."

So what does all this mean? First of all, Patrick is likely smiling in his new, young, handsome body. He's relishing the fact that since his death, I have become substantially more introspective. I've become much more observant and willing to examine my own thoughts and feelings.

When I think of "reprieve" and "freedom," I can't help but think of all the responsibility I shouldered during the decline of both of my parents and my brother, how I was literally in charge of everything, how I was simultaneously a student and a conductor. Truthfully, it was a lot. Perhaps after they all died and the required legal work was handled, I felt a reprieve.

Freedom? Perhaps as I no longer have a family member whose health is of concern to me, I feel free. Throughout our years together, Patrick had substantially more health challenges than I. He was conscientious about his health, so I never felt it was my job to keep track of it, but I certainly felt a high level of concern.

If I could magically have him back, believe me, I would gladly carry whatever level of concern and responsibility was necessary to keep him healthy and by my side.

11

The East Coast Gentleman

This relationship is a great demonstration of the value of meeting someone sooner rather than later, and for me, it shows why I prefer to meet someone who lives nearby.

Developing a relationship over a long distance is tough. Distance creates pressure. People put their best foot forward—something anyone can do for a short period. But it's not an accurate reflection of who they are on a day-to-day basis. In the meantime, there is distance and only sporadic in-person rendezvous.

Even if someone says they are willing to move, they're not going to do so until there's a strong bond in place and the move makes sense. In addition, a big move puts pressure on the person who is staying put to incorporate the new person into their life, show them the sights, introduce them to people, and help them get situated in a completely new environment.

Joseph and I chatted via text, then phone, and then Zoom for two months. He was a widower, so talk was easy, natural, and non-judgmental. Over this time, we developed quite a strong connection, believing that we had a lot in common—beliefs, values, the importance of family, and hopes for the future.

I was very clear about the need to meet face-to-face. Would there be any chemistry? Would our activity levels and interests be compatible?

Joseph flew from the East Coast to Seattle for a four-day weekend and stayed in a downtown hotel. We shared multiple meals, went for a strenuous walk, attended a concert at T-Mobile Park (great seats on the floor), and talked and talked.

While I enjoyed our chats, it was clear early on that I was considerably more active and in better shape than he was. To be fair, he was a couple of years older than me. He was also quite close to my height, and as petty as this may sound, I prefer a taller man.

At the end of the four days, he asked the inevitable question. "Well, what do you think? Are you open to continuing this relationship?" As uncomfortable as it was to speak my truth, I said, "No, I just don't feel any chemistry, and that is important to me. Perhaps I am spoiled, as my connection to Patrick was immediate and electric. I know it's not fair, and I'm trying hard not to make comparisons. Maybe I'm just not ready."

He argued that chemistry builds over time, but for me, that wasn't likely to happen. Truly a delightful, gracious, generous, and thoughtful man. But not for me.

JOURNALING DAY 6

How am I taking care of myself?

I just returned from a ninety-minute massage—some much-needed attention to my touch-deprived, somewhat stress-filled body. That is kindness.

Kindness is knowing that I need to take care of myself in this uncharted territory. It's doing the simple things like taking a shower, getting plenty of rest, getting some exercise, and eating healthy food. (Not sure my dinner of potato chips and wine really counts, though.) It's also allowing myself to be pampered—manicure, facial, haircut, massage, the works.

On the more demanding side, kindness is putting aside my inner critic, dropping the "shoulds," and letting go of all judgments (especially the self-judgments). Kindness is spending time with people willing to gently hold space for me and be okay with the awkward moments. It's surrounding myself with nurturing, not toxic, people. It's finding my tribe. It's allowing myself to experience whatever emotion presents itself at any given moment. To know that it is all okay, as there is no right or wrong way to "do" grief.

Kindness is also encouraging myself to reach out and ask for help. To give myself permission. More often than not, I honestly don't know what I need. But when it's something I don't know how to do, it's quite okay to admit that and believe that helping me will probably give someone else great joy.

Kindness is paying attention to myself in the moment, listening to my thoughts and feelings, and trusting that I know what's best.

12
Mr. Patient and Persistent

I was approached online by a man who lives in Oregon. He was a widower who had nursed his wife for years before her passing, and our interests certainly aligned. I told myself that pursuing relationships across state lines was ridiculous. But since I was driving to Oregon to visit my brother-in-law, I thought, *Why not meet this guy for a drink?*

We chatted for several hours, comfortable and relaxed. I later learned that he thought we had an immediate, strong connection that was destined for success. Jumping to that conclusion seemed precipitous and premature to me.

Unless I am immediately drawn to someone, it takes me a while to warm up. Over the next few months, we chatted on the phone and continued to learn more about each other.

In August, I planned to travel to the Oregon coast with my daughter and two other women friends to visit the inn where Patrick had died. I wanted to plant a bleeding heart in his honor.

The people at the inn were very gracious, offering hors d'oeuvres and wine after we completed the ceremony I had planned.

I had intended to meet up with David earlier in the summer when I returned from my travels to Ireland and Norway, but I was not feeling well and knew it was best to cancel. Instead, I arranged to connect with him after our group completed our stay at the inn and traveled our separate ways.

I offered to drive to his house to join him for dinner and spend the night, making sure that I could have my own bedroom and bathroom before agreeing to do so.

During that visit, I learned some important things. David's verbal behavior was often stream-of-consciousness. Every thought that flowed through his brain was expressed with vivid details that were often of no interest to me. Initially, I was willing to attribute this practice to nerves, but over time, I believed otherwise.

He was a sommelier of sorts and had an amazing collection of wines plus a beautiful garden and a large home that required constant attention. David loved to travel, a passion we shared; he was financially stable and definitely enjoyed spoiling me.

He took me on a three-day vacation east of the mountains, where I ignited his determination to learn tennis and pickleball. We also went on a seven-day vacation to Hawaii with a number of his friends who had traveled many times with him and his wife while she was able to do so. Before I agreed to go on either of these adventures, I told him that I had to have my own bedroom and bathroom. I also was very clear that if he had a woman in his life who was likely to be more romantic (read "sexually open") than I was, he should definitely invite her instead. But—off we went.

Although David has made several moves, I have remained relatively steadfast. His generosity is unsurpassed. He is kind and we share the same political mindset. And I must say that his continued pursuit of me does not feel pushy or intrusive whatsoever. He's gentle and respectful. There may be another visit to Oregon in my future.

JOURNALING DAY 7

What was one way you showed your love for Patrick?

Once in a while, I wrote a poem for him, though that was not a natural form of expression for me. Some of my creations surprised me. Here is a poem that I wrote to Patrick on August 7, 2008, on the occasion of our twenty-seventh anniversary.

27 street legal

My lover and life partner

Confidante and companion

Architect of my heart

Your eyes quietly noting the ripples of my soul

Sensing the softness, the gentle flow

Cautiously curious, tempted to expand

With a loving nudge, you invite me to step forward

To explore beyond the safe confines of success

To wrestle with the unhewn edges of creativity

Gently massaging my warm cocoon

Offering delicate wings for yet another flight

Encouraging me to cultivate my mirrored image

Along for the unpredictable ride

My heart bursts with blessings

So grateful to travel this path with you

13
The Northerner

This is an extremely difficult chapter to write. I'll call "The Northerner" Michael.

I will love Michael for the rest of my life. No matter what, I will carry him in my heart. He saved me from numbness. He saved me from withering. He is like my personal automated external defibrillator.

And—he is the man I hate to love.

Michael and I met at a reception close to a year ago. He and his older woman companion sat right in front of me and my friend. While we were waiting for the speaker to begin, the four of us started to chat. The electric charge I felt in my body was immediate and palpable. Only the two of us understood what we said to each other. By the end of the session, phone numbers had been exchanged—interestingly, at the request of the older woman.

The only other person in my life with whom I've experienced that strong a connection so quickly was Patrick. When I talked with Patrick the first time, I felt like my soul knew his soul, that we shared an indescribably deep connection, one that made me believe

I had known him in a previous life. Months into our relationship, he shared that he had felt the same way. I wasn't alone. I wasn't crazy.

Connecting with Michael was not the same in that regard. But I did feel the electricity, the chemistry, the excitement. For four years, I had felt dead, unable to feel a sense of joy in a man's company. Fun, yes; electricity, no. Now I knew it was possible. And for that, I am eternally grateful.

Months have passed, and even now, I can't tell you what kind of relationship we have. I can't define it. I think I do know, however, that it is not healthy for me. That's my head talking. My heart feels differently, and consequently, it continues to get crushed. I actually thought some romance was budding between us. Looking back, I think I fooled myself. Nights of hunger, unfulfilled.

Michael says communication is critical to him, but he's horrible at it. His communication is vague, erratic, often consisting of a pithy one liner, and can be obtuse or sarcastic. I can't say that he is healthy—mentally, emotionally, or physically. He has suffered trauma, neither resolved nor successfully addressed, and has a number of health-related challenges.

I have tried in vain to encourage, help, and support him, and nudge him toward better health. But there is no follow through on his part. As Patrick used to say, "You can't worry about somebody more than they worry about themselves." Of course, he was right.

Michael has to decide for himself that it's time to focus and make some changes.

Interestingly, as I said earlier, I will always love him, and Michael feels similarly. He once said to me, "Our meeting was meant to be. The health challenges I was about to face would have killed me had I not had our relationship."

"For that," he added, "I will always love you."

Michael's life is complicated. He is inextricably attached to this older woman, not romantically, but rather more as a financial overseer/caretaker/companion. She wields a lot of control and power over him, which he allows, then fights, and then allows again, eternally stuck on this merry-go-round.

I am a doer; he's a procrastinator. I lean liberal; he leans conservative and traditional. I value my health and am very active; so far, that's not the case with him. I believe in straightforward, honest, and open communication. He says he does so too, but he doesn't practice it. He has a number of narcissistic tendencies. I don't believe I do.

So what's the attraction? Believe me, I have asked myself that question a million times. He's not even my type physically.

I find Michael intellectually stimulating. While we are interested in very different things, I continue to learn from him. Some of that knowledge is and will continue to be helpful in my life. He is mysterious and challenging, both of those qualities being double-edged swords. He makes me laugh, honest-to-goodness belly laughs. And his enveloping hugs provide strength, warmth, and safety. Patrick's hugs were like that too.

His charming, infectious ways cajoled me into entering his old RV, one of his many vehicles, in the parking lot of a restaurant. That might be up there as one of the most unexpected things I've ever done, even when I think back to my the years of my youth. There I was, naked and enveloped by a man with a giant cock, being lovingly and gently touched for the first time in years. Since Patrick died, Michael is the only man for whom I have taken off my clothes.

Since I still have some medical problems after my emergency hysterectomy, it's good to know that there are many ways to express affection for someone. I'm glad I know a few of those. More homework in store.

My feelings were visceral. After years of feeling numb, it was exciting to have actual bodily sensations. My skin craved the touch. I soaked up every gentle stroke. How I missed being held. How I missed someone caring about me, wanting to be with me. I had a fleeting moment of self-doubt, feeling like I was jumping the gun, full throttle and no brakes. But the truth is—I didn't care. Every part of me was hungry. Every part of me ached with need. Not desperation, just need and desire.

The power over which I seemingly, or thus far, have little control is like a neodymium magnetic pull (an iron–boron magnet, the strongest you can buy). I don't understand it.

So how do I get my head and my heart in alignment? This is quite an interesting enigma and experience for me. Sometimes, the psychologist cannot "heal" herself.

Clearly, I'm projecting qualities onto him that I want him to have, qualities that are important to me. I keep waiting for the impossible. He is who he is. He has the issues he has. I can't wish them away. I can't "fix" him. With the passage of time, I know I *must* let him go.

I recently had a dream that I was outside in gorgeous sunshine, hiking with Michael. We were both smiling, laughing, and absolutely delighted by our peaceful surroundings. As I rounded a bend on the trail, Patrick appeared in front of me with arms outstretched to give me a gigantic hug. I turned, confused, to look behind me. Michael was gone.

Honestly, I'm struggling with this one. Is Patrick reminding me of his love and all we had, making Michael disappear? Or is Michael my "next Patrick"? My head knows that's a resounding *no*.

In another dream, Patrick and I were in a car. He reached over and put his hand down my pants trying to stroke my butt, saying, "I have fallen in love with you forever." Funny—I can imagine Michael doing that as well. Not saying those words but doing *that*.

People have asked what inspired me to write this book. I believe it was Michael and how I felt when I was with him. I felt alive. I felt joyful. I felt challenged, and I felt a sense of hunger that, for years, had been totally absent. I also felt intense disappointment. What's important, though, is that I actually felt *something!* For that, I am thankful.

JOURNALING DAY 8

As I struggle to move forward on this path of recovery, who is my wisest counsel?

She who is with me 24/7 is my wisest, most reliable, and consistent counsel. She who reminds me to breathe, who gently suggests I unfurl that clenched fist, who stays by my side in the darkness, and who hears my heart and assures me that I will be okay.

She, who would be I . . . knows death.

I worked at our local trauma center. I'm a certified health advocate and navigator; I've taught workshops to help people talk about and outline their end-of-life wishes and understand the medical choices available to them.

I lost my father, mother, and only sibling between 2006 and 2008. Cardiac failure, Alzheimer's, and prostate cancer, respectively.

What I don't know and what I don't understand is traumatic loss—the sudden and unexpected loss of a loved one, and what it's like to never say goodbye, to feel so caught off-guard and unprepared. Can I trust myself to find my way? Now, I have to learn. This is the supreme test. Answers and guidance come in bits and pieces.

So I bumble on. One day at a time, one step at a time, exploring land I never asked to see. I reach for lifelines when I'm flailing. I'm learning to find joy in the unexpected and look forward to feeling it again. I remind myself to find moments of grace and gratitude, to not waste what I have. And all the while, I keep looking for the rudder that will guide me and the wind that will move me forward.

14

Purposeful Self-Care

After Patrick died, I muddled around on my own for a while, quite sure I could handle all the grief by myself. After all, as a psychologist who had spent so many years focused on death and dying, I should be able to do this. Right?

Wrong!

I joined a group online (remember, it was COVID times) and quickly realized it wasn't for me. The group members had been meeting for a long time and knew each other well. Furthermore, none of them had experienced a traumatic loss. I felt like an interloper.

I switched gears and went in for two private sessions with a grief therapist. Again, not for me. She and I were not a good match. I needed someone who was going to challenge me, nudge me, ask difficult questions. I didn't need a grandma type saying, "There, there, everything is going to be fine."

I finally found a traumatic loss grief group. *That* was a fit. There were only five of us in the group plus a psychologist and a chaplain intern. Participating in that group was well worth my time. The five of us learned from each other, understood the pain we all shared, and began to embrace our own loss with love.

Just a note here: *It's important to take the time to choose the best group or therapist to meet your needs. This is not the time to worry about someone else's feelings if you decide to move in a different direction. You will know when you find the best place to start addressing your pain and grief.*

Once the traumatic loss group was over, I struck out on my own, stubborn optimist that I am, believing I had the tools to survive.

I woke up one morning with the realization that everyone was pissing me off. I felt angry, frustrated, and short-tempered. Knowing that is not my true nature, I finally admitted that seeing a trauma therapist, one on one, might be in my best interest.

That was a good decision—again, well worth my time. I grew to understand that my job was to focus on the grief process—*my* process. And the goal was not to essentially get over it. I worked on forgiving myself, on understanding how my sense of safety had been damaged, on the relationship between fear and grief, how to let go of the need to control, and how to relax my need to achieve. I learned to appreciate my stability, my ability to balance mood with mindfulness, and my resiliency.

After working with the therapist for about a year, I realized I needed and wanted to create more "purpose" in my life. My website was still up and running, but I was actually doing very little consulting. For the most part, I was available and happy to help friends but the active marketer in me had lost her drive.

Just like I had sought out the most appropriate support, whether in the form of a group or an individual therapist, I embarked on a trial-and-error search for a rewarding way to contribute. I volunteered with the Make-a-Wish Foundation but soon realized that while it was an outstanding organization, it was not the right fit for me, at least not at that time.

For the last three years, I have volunteered my service and time to Crisis Connections, our local crisis line. After completing a thorough and in-depth ten-week training program, I started responding to callers.

As someone who prides herself on her creative imagination, I never cease to be amazed at the variety of situations people find themselves in or that they create. The stories and situations I hear, coupled with the experiences I had working in a trauma hospital, make the periodic tumultuousness of my life seem mild and manageable.

There's a lot to be learned from perspective.

I truly enjoy the work at the clinic. It aligns with my skills, it's highly varied, and I feel good about my ability to hold space for people and provide support, along with guiding them to other helpful resources. Now, in addition to answering the phone line,

I serve as one of the trainers for new volunteers. That, too, is rewarding.

Another way I've added meaning to my life is by serving as a facilitator for a spousal loss grief group for over a year. Only recently did I decide I needed a break from that work. Suddenly, seeing people face-to-face, witnessing their pain in the early stages of loss felt heavy to me. Perhaps the combination of the group members' physical presence, the pain of their expressions, and their body language became overwhelming. Whether or not I will return to the group remains unknown.

Through these avenues, I believe I am making a difference. I hope this is part of my legacy when it is my turn to transition.

JOURNALING DAY 9

What was the first thing that attracted me to Patrick?

Oh, those baby blues. Like magnets, they drew me in. There was no resisting. They held me. Captivated me. Simultaneously, they pierced my heart, allowing him to quickly explore my deepest being. I fear those baby blues know me better than I know myself.

Sitting on that park bench and eating lunch . . . our first conversation. I was entranced, confused, and scared.

Have I met you? Do I know you? I know I know those eyes. The depth of your wisdom, the power of your love, the warmth of your arms. I've been here before. Traveled worlds and lifetimes with you.

I think I'm home.

15

The Spineless Ghost

While I was busy hiking in the canyons of the Southwest, I connected online with a Seattle guy whom I'll call Ghost. On the second day of texting, we decided to have a chat over the phone. Clearly, I felt comfortable and trusting enough that I broke my own rule of not sharing personal information—no phone numbers, no email addresses—until I'd met someone face to face.

We spoke for an hour, during which it became clear that we shared many of the same interests, values, and beliefs. I was happy to have something to look forward to when I returned to Seattle.

While the text exchange continued, there were no more phone calls until I was back home. Our next direct chat was at 10 p.m. one night. Given the nature of the call, it was pretty clear that we were both excited to meet. Maybe a little too excited. Ghost said, "I'm coming over. I can be there in twenty minutes."

I was a bit incredulous. "Now? It's almost eleven!" That was immaterial to him. At that point, I said something that even surprised me. "Before you get in the car, you need to know we are not going to bed together."

On a side note, I've had some interesting discussions about sex with my daughter and her best friend. I'm clearly old-fashioned and not interested in being intimate with someone without an emotional connection. I can't just act because someone is attractive. I need substance and trust, both of which take time to establish. I've learned this is called demisexuality—where a person feels sexually attracted to someone only after they've developed a close emotional bond with them.

So, back to Ghost. He did come to visit. The energy we both felt on the phone played out in person, in a "controlled" way. I held to my rule. He was a handsome man with whom I had a lot in common. It was clear we would continue to get acquainted.

Over time, however, my frustration grew as Ghost would commit to getting back to me and not follow through. He ran his own technology business and worked excessive hours, as many in high-tech do. That said, one of my pet peeves is not sticking to your commitments. If you can't follow through on a prior appointment, at least communicate that. Don't leave people hanging. It's rude and disrespectful.

I saw Ghost in person one more time. We sat in his car at a waterfront park and chatted for hours. Topics included relationships—what works and what doesn't for each of us—and politics, a topic on which we saw eye to eye. This was all before the 2024 elections.

I thought this relationship had legs. I thought it could grow into something good. I never thought Ghost would just disappear without a word.

To this day, I grapple with understanding this kind of behavior, how someone can decide to quietly fade away. It doesn't take much effort to just say, "This isn't working for me. Thanks for your time. I hope you meet someone with whom you share happiness." Is it really that hard?

So there you have the Spineless Ghost.

JOURNALING DAY 10

How do I feel about all the emotions I'm experiencing? Do they frighten me?

I'm not afraid of emotions, pretty much any of them. I just don't want to get stuck anywhere, to feel like I can't crawl out of a hole or away from the unbearable. No, I don't turn my back on those feelings. I just don't want to wallow in them. And yes, I'm willing to spend whatever amount of time and effort is needed to tackle these feelings so I can eventually move forward and dedicate that energy elsewhere.

I have always been someone who likes provocative films: the ones that make me think; the ones that offer perspective. Patrick used to say I liked the darkness.

I believe life is about contrast and emotions are a continuum. I need to understand the darkness and the gloom in order to recognize and appreciate the light, elation, and joy. I like the phrase "overcome by neither; open to both." Melancholy would not be my middle name. Melancholy is gloominess. That's different than sorrow.

I hated yesterday. I couldn't wait for it to be over. My first Thanksgiving (the first of many firsts) without Patrick in forty years. I sobbed for hours. Cradling Patrick's ashes, I swayed to "Don't Know Much" by Linda Ronstadt and Aaron Neville and "Endless Love" by Lionel Richie and Diana Ross. Guaranteed to lead to tears every time. Perhaps some would call this melancholy. More aptly, I was wailing, keening. A much more active version of gloom than what the word "melancholy" suggests.

16
Otherworldly Phenomena

I believe in staying open to messages from other realms. There are times I can feel Patrick around me. It may be a flash of light that quickly draws my attention and then disappears. It may be a sound that appears out of nowhere and makes no sense.

On my first birthday weekend after Patrick's death, my cousin and his partner came to visit from Los Angeles and stayed the weekend. Two strange things happened while they were here. They witnessed them. I didn't just imagine them.

We were preparing breakfast and had placed three plates on the counter. The plates clattered as if one had been resting, ever so slightly, on the edge of another and then fallen to a level position. But no one had touched the plates, and they had never been resting on each other.

The night before, after we came home from dinner, I asked Siri to turn on the lights. About thirty seconds later, out of the blue, Siri started playing "Come Away with Me" by Norah Jones, one of Patrick's favorites. We all looked at each other incredulously. Patrick was with us, no question.

Another example: One day while driving to meet a neurosurgical nurse with whom I used to work, I was listening to a webinar by a spiritual teacher and medium based in California. His presentation gave me chills, up and down my body. I saved his name, deciding that he would be the person I'd contact if I ever decided to take the plunge and try a medium.

Six months after Patrick died, I did just that. As I write this now, I have tears in my eyes. I just replayed the recording of my session, as it's been quite a while since I'd heard it. This medium is phenomenal. I told him nothing. Truly nothing. As a bit of a skeptic, I wanted to see what he would come up with.

The reading was astounding. I came away feeling as if I had just spoken with Patrick. As the medium connected with Patrick, he was able to relate that I had lost my husband of many, many years very unexpectedly, that his death had come out of nowhere and turned my world upside down. He related that Patrick had fallen, hit his head, and grabbed his chest.

He talked about Patrick's entrepreneurial initiatives, that we had a son and a daughter and what was going on in each of their lives, the challenges each of them was facing. He knew I was doing something with Patrick's wedding ring, that it was going to be altered in some way. I had given it to our son as he was getting married. He made a stylish modification to the ring to make it his and will always wear it, forever carrying his father's essence.

The medium relayed that Patrick was proud of both of our kids and that he wanted to reassure our daughter about the changes she was going through, to be there to catch her and be her protector. And he relished the relationship he had with our son, "a mini me." Or, as I often say, our son is Patrick Version 2.0.

Next, the medium assured me that he honors the strong bond we built as a family and encourages us to protect and nurture what we have. To keep it going.

Toward the session's end, the medium shared that he has done a lot of these readings and that this one was an honor. That we, as a family, have created such love and closeness. Nothing can break the bond we have.

JOURNALING DAY 11

How do I feel about the journey I'm on?

I'm tired of writing. I'm tired of hurting. I'm tired. Just tired.

I feel dead inside. Like someone put me on "mute" or "pause." I feel isolated and alone in my own nothingness. I'm like a kid with a tantrum. I don't like this. NO! NO! NO! I don't want to. I want to go back. Why can't things be the same as they were? Go away. No, don't. Leave me alone. No, don't.

I feel like Kaavan, the world's loneliest elephant.

17
Taking Some Risks

Two flying leaps. Thankfully, both turned out to be quite safe.

Flying Leap Number One: I attended a neuroscience fundraiser before Christmas. I've always said that if I had my life to do over, I'd become a neurosurgeon, an MD instead of a PhD. Alas, that's not going to happen. Instead, I do all I can to continue learning.

Anyway, I attended this fundraiser with one of my former employees. I dressed for the occasion and, if I do say so myself, I looked good. At the table next to ours, I noticed a handsome guy with a dashing head of hair. My first thought was "surfer dude." We checked each other out a few times, but that was it until I was out on the street waiting for a valet to retrieve my car. Mr. Surfer walked toward me and, much to my surprise, I said something along the lines of, "I just want to run my fingers through your hair." He laughed, and we started talking. His name was Shawn.

Shawn commented on how truly elegant I looked and how beautifully I carried myself. He asked me where I was from; I laughed and answered with the name of the neighborhood about ten minutes from where we stood. He asked where that was—my first clue he wasn't a local. Good hunch on my part. He was from California, a haven for surfing.

Shawn suggested we go get a drink. I pondered on that and said, "Why don't you just come to my place. I have plenty of wine and liquor." Risky, right? But by then, I knew his occupation and how he was connected with the event, so I felt pretty safe.

As much as I trust my gut, my husband always used to say I did not have enough Spidey sense. He was from Detroit and never sat with his back to a door. But, in this case, I trusted my intuition and off we went to my place.

This was definitely a rapid connection that could have easily led to the bedroom had I been game. This was probably what he was expecting since I had boldly offered my place instead of a bar. But again, I'm not a one-and-done kind of person, and I didn't know if I'd ever see this man again, so my answer was, "No, not happening."

We had a great time, great conversation, and great kisses. That said, I had him call an Uber several hours later and return to his hotel.

P.S. We shared a few texts but haven't seen each other since. So thankful I was true to myself.

Flying Leap Number Two: Another entertaining text exchange with a man whose profile listed his age as fifty-two.

After returning home at 7 p.m. from a happy hour meetup, one that I have not yet shared here, I thought, "Hey, the night is young, why not reach out to this fifty-two-year-old guy and see if he's up for a glass of wine?" The risk? I suggested he just come to my place.

Brad got himself all ready, showered, shaved, and walked out the door only to discover he had a flat tire. Trip aborted. Or so we thought. Not to be deterred, he found a neighbor with a Fix-A-Flat solution, repaired the tire, and reported that he was on his way.

When Brad arrived, he parked in my garage and we wandered toward the elevator. As I looked at him more carefully now, I wondered, *Fifty-two? Nope, no way.* Turned out he was thirty-seven! Brad could almost be my grandson.

It's surprising how many young men say they like older women. Do they think I'm a sugar mama? Do they wonder what it would be like to sleep with an older woman? Are they looking for more wisdom? Are they just full of BS? Too late. Brad was here, and he certainly was charming.

Our conversation didn't flow easily or naturally. Rather, it was work. I felt like Brad's counselor/therapist/grandmother asking him what he really planned to do with his life. We had skydiving in common, an unusual angle, but that was about it.

Yet, the man seemed to be quite taken by me. Feels a bit foolish to admit that but the way he positioned himself so close to me when I refilled our wine glasses made his intentions very clear. After about two hours, I ushered him toward the door. Time to go. But he wasn't leaving without a kiss. Confession: What a great kiss!

He sent me a text shortly after leaving. "It was so lovely meeting you. I'm on cloud nine! I can't wait to see you again, really! My tire is good, still holding air. Although I have to admit part of me was hoping that my tire would be flat so that I'd get to stay back with you. I'd love to see you again. I can smell your perfume on me and it's intoxicating."

Not surprisingly, Brad was already angling for another rendezvous. While there was a tiny bit of intrigue on my part, I came to my senses pretty soon. The whole thing was ridiculous, unless I was just looking for a fling.

I passed. But I *do* still think of him. It was such a good kiss!

JOURNALING DAY 12

How is my pain affecting me?

I don't need to *look* for pain. That "smoldering ache of loss" is etched into my soul, embedded in my heart. It's nestling into every crevice of my body, looking for a permanent place to live. Somedays I think it's quite greedy, demanding more space, time, and energy than I want to share. Maybe once I learn to live with this new companion, acknowledge and honor it, it will relax its smothering grip as well as its need for mental and emotional space.

Sometimes I think Patrick is lucky. He can ignore the pervasiveness of global pain. He is not faced with numbing, exhausting grief. He is not busy trying to put this thousand-piece puzzle of his heart back together, only to realize that he's missing some pieces.

Thank goodness for my handful of friends who hold space for me, sit with my tears, and embrace my pain rather than attempt to dissipate it. Thank goodness for my own willingness to be vulnerable with a chosen few. And thank goodness for deciding to share my feelings through written words rather than trying to articulate them through speech, over and over and over.

I can hear my heart and can sit with myself in the darkness. She continues to assure me I'm going to be okay. *Patience, sweetheart, patience.*

18

A Conundrum

I met Lewis online a number of months ago. We met at a coffee shop and proceeded to take a walk along the beach. Our primary shared interest was music. Nice enough chat, nice enough guy, no sparks per se but enough interest that we shared phone numbers.

But after that, radio silence.

A number of months later, he reached out online, obviously having forgotten that we had connected once before. He asked about meeting up again, so we met for happy hour drinks. Interestingly, I had a very different feeling this time. I felt a lot more compatibility, more interest, and more curiosity. Likewise from his end.

Why the change? I had to ask myself. What was different? Had I really not been paying attention the first time? Was I just more open now? Had I not been ready for a relationship before? I had no answers but was determined to keep an open mind.

Several weeks later, Lewis and I met for a light meal and a jazz performance. The conversation flowed. Plenty to talk about, thoughts and plans to explore, and jazz to enjoy. We shared a warm hug at the end of the night and said our goodbyes.

I traveled out of state shortly thereafter to visit my son and his wife. While I was gone, Lewis and I traded several texts through which he discovered that I had met many famous classical musicians when I was younger, as both my parents were accomplished and well known in the music scene. Lewis seemed blown away that I was rather cavalier about having met these professionals and had even played ping-pong with a few.

And then came another disappearing act. Lewis quietly faded away for a while, though sometime later, he wrote to say how nice it was to meet me. Frankly, I didn't feel strongly enough about him to question his sudden disappearing act. I'm not shy so I certainly would have queried him about it had I been motivated to do so.

I still don't understand why some people just go dark. Again, how much courage does it take to write a text saying thanks but no thanks? Not much.

JOURNALING DAY 13

How do my friends fit into my journey? How do they "see" me?

How do people see me? I'm not sure I care. Perhaps they see me as pathetic. Perhaps they feel sorry for me. Perhaps they are tongue-tied. Most cannot begin to imagine the reality of a sudden, totally unexpected death, of not being able to say goodbye. Of my love of forty years leaving my side. Poof!

Part of my challenge is to figure out who can sit with me, hold space for me, and allow me to grieve, who will ask how I am doing—right now, this minute—and can handle the response. I have one dear friend who said, "I want to be part of this trek. I will be patient and always appreciative of the chance to be allowed into your heart and soul as you grieve." She is a blessing.

I have always been the one encouraging people to talk about death and dying, stressing the importance of creating a clear and specific advance healthcare directive, doing the work while you are physically and mentally capable. While you can think clearly and are not in crisis. The goal is to recognize that death is part of life, and the more we know about and understand death, the more comfortable we are with it.

An advance healthcare directive is a living will. It's a legal document in which you authorize a healthcare advocate, whom you have selected, to speak on your behalf should you not be able to do so yourself. The document outlines the medical treatments you want and/or don't want and instructions about your future medical care.

Given how difficult it is to convince people to do this work, it's clear there is still tremendous discomfort around the topic of death.

My friends know I know death. I certainly know it intellectually. And I know it emotionally. At least I thought I did. But I did not know what it feels like to be stabbed in the heart, to feel gut-wrenching distress, to walk around with a vomit bag for ten days. No—that was not a pain I had known before.

Am I wiser now? Do I have an even greater understanding of and appreciation for impermanence and non-attachment? Indeed. Do people recognize that? I don't know and I still don't care. How *I* feel is what's most important!

19

Some Kind of Coincidence

I am not using real names of the men whose stories I'm sharing. I've given each one an alias. There's one, however, whose story is short and whose parallels to my life almost defy belief.

His real name? Patrick. That feels uncanny from the get-go. Patrick and I began to chat through a dating site; I learned that his wife had died in 2020, the same year as my husband. His wife's name? Pam!

We had to meet. The similarities were too eerie to ignore. One meeting is all it took. Although he was financially stable, owned a boat, and had a partnership in a small plane, none of that mattered. He was a staunch Trump supporter, an advocate for a presidential candidate whose narcissism and moral character are unacceptable to me. Politics really can be a dividing factor.

In addition, he was short and unattractive. There was nothing promising about him. No chance for an "us." My curiosity was satisfied. We never met again.

JOURNALING DAY 14

How does my "space" feel without Patrick's presence?

I am not in a new home or town. Unless you want to call my living space "new" in the sense that you're not here. Is it "new" because I can see and feel you in every corner and am sure you are going to walk through the door but really . . . you're not here? Sometimes I hallucinate, see a flash of light, or am startled by a sound. But still, you're not here.

You know every square inch of where I live. Somehow this quote by Nabokov feels apropos today: "The cradle rocks above an abyss, and common sense tells us that our existence is but a brief crack of light between two eternities of darkness."

There was so much more light for us to discover. So much more light to explore. You said you weren't ready to go. Then why did you?

Take my hand. Travel with me to feel the warmth of the light. Come fill this space.

20
Yup, a Judgment

Years ago, when Patrick and I bought a condo in San Diego, and almost simultaneously traded in the home where we had raised our kids for a Seattle condo, I got this funny feeling in the pit of my stomach that this was the beginning of the end. Somehow, owning a condo rather than a home seemed like we were admitting our age, that we were definitely getting older. A ridiculous thought, I know.

So when I ended up on a couple of dates with George, a man who had decided to sell his home with a beautiful garden and move into a retirement facility, I immediately thought, "Oh no, this guy is way too old for me." In truth, he was perhaps two years older at most.

The best part of seeing George was having a drink, after visiting a museum, at a lovely hotel bar where I was introduced to the concept of adding elderflower to my lemon drop. In that relaxed environment, we had a good talk. He even commented that it was our best conversation yet.

A week or so later, George suggested we go to a movie and then out to dinner. Initially, I agreed, but days later, when I got honest with myself, I changed my mind. I knew in my heart that this couldn't develop into a meaningful relationship, and the thought of visiting him in a retirement facility turned my stomach.

When I told him gently that I didn't want to see him again, he bitterly proclaimed that he had been quite patient with me, likely referring to the fact that I had resisted all of his advances.

Granted, it's not comfortable to be rejected by someone, but it's certainly worse to live a lie.

JOURNALING DAY 15

What am I learning about myself as I travel this rocky road filled with potholes?

Writing these journal entries is grueling work. One more thing to do. And yes, like in the case of homework, I know in my heart that there is so much to learn from engaging in this exercise.

Ha! I just had a flashback about dissecting a frog. Talk about the Wayback Machine! That was a junior high exercise. I was disgusted. Didn't want to touch it. It was tough enough to just look at this dead frog. But, as the teacher had instructed us, I needed to take a deep breath and dissect the frog, one step at a time. If I needed a break between each step, I could walk away, look out the window, talk to a friend, and take more deep breaths. But I did need to return to the table and keep going. Ultimately, I had to admit there was value in examining this frog and its guts from so many angles.

The grief continuum is substantially bigger, longer, and deeper than I had imagined. The branches of the continuum can be confusing, scary, or just dead ends. Some days, I feel like a petulant child, irritated at things that truly don't matter, unwilling to let go, to let things be. Some days I feel corpulent, every move demanding effort, but like a good soldier, I traipse through the sludge and make myself take a step. Keep working on that frog.

So what am I learning?

The older I get, the more I know I can't control. There is immense value in giving myself permission to feel, explore, and let things evolve on their own. To admit that I can't push the river.

Practice self-care, accept each emotion as it shows up, admit this is way more complicated than I thought (or perhaps hoped for), be *patient*, and know it's okay to ask for help.

The major work is mine to do and I must trust myself to do it. At each "stage" of the grieving process, the ways of most effectively doing that work might change. Be open to exploring different modalities, different processes, different approaches. Undoubtedly, answers to questions will change over time as awareness morphs and knowledge increases.

Bottom line: I need to love, care for, and trust myself. And be patient! Redundant advice, I know. But maybe if I continue to say this and hear this and write this, I'll internalize it someday.

21
Somehow Just Creepy

I had a coffee date with a man with whom I went to high school (I didn't know him back then). I waited thirty minutes at the coffee shop. He never showed. Close to eleven hours later, I received a text from Dan saying he'd left home without the exact address of the coffee shop, that he'd walked all around the area he thought it was in. He had even gone to the library to look up coffee shops in the neighborhood. Not until eleven hours later did I receive a half-hearted "sorry" in a text message.

Then he begged for another chance!

Obviously, his tech devices are not synched, and he's clearly disorganized and impolite. Of course, I refused.

Months later, Dan contacted me again. I reminded him of our previous non-rendezvous. Guess I have to add "bad memory" to that man's list of issues. He told me he was attending an upcoming gathering of our high school peers and that I was certainly welcome to join him at the party. I decided to attend but told him I'd get there on my own. This would give me an opportunity to maybe see some old friends and also meet Dan in a group setting.

Brilliant decision on my part. Two of the women at the party had this to say about Dan: "Stay away!" They were adamant. "Don't get involved. Dan is bad news." There did seem to be something creepy about him. Maybe he was more annoying than creepy, given how he declared himself a member of MENSA. You'd never know it.

When it was time for me to leave, I felt compelled to lie to escape the inevitable question of, "May I call you?"

"No. I'm sorry," I hurried to say. "I'm actually seeing someone."

JOURNALING DAY 16

How do I plan to navigate this life on my own? How do I feel about the need to do just that?

I see the migrant children put in cages at the border. They arrived in our country with people they trusted, people who believed they would finally be able to live without constantly fearing for their lives. A land of opportunity, a place where they could be safe, grow, and prosper. A land where they would be surrounded by people who respected them, people who gave them a chance.

Instead, without a hint of warning, the children have been ripped from the arms of their loved ones. They have no understanding of what just happened or why. They believe that their loved ones will be back, scoop them up in their arms, keep them warm, and calm them with affectionate whispers. They have no reason not to. They don't know any better.

Meanwhile, they are screaming. They are scared. They are cold. They are hungry. Every once in a while, they play a game with another child, share some laughter, and mute their pain and sorrow. But only for a short time.

There is so much they don't understand. Why are they being treated as they are and what happened to all those promises of a good life?

How do they navigate this world of unknowns? Figure out how to survive? I wonder if they want to.

So many broken hearts. Theirs and mine.

22

A Collection of Undesirables

S ome men I've met on the dating scene deserve to be put in the same box. Open the box quickly, add another name and another saga, and close it. Done.

- The night I played happy hour therapist with a married but separated man who had lots of unfinished business with his wife and their relationship. His search for a new partner was quite premature.

- The unkempt man who looked like he hadn't showered in a week.

- The man who first went to the wrong restaurant, finally arrived at the place we were supposed to meet, and literally slobbered into his food. Frankly, I was embarrassed to be seen with him.

- The guys who disappeared because I wouldn't give them my phone number or email address before I'd gotten to know them, preferably face-to-face.

- Long-distance impossibilities: The man from Kona, Hawaii, who asked if I like younger men. The one from Deer Park, New York, who said, "I like your face."

- The local guy who wrote, "You look great but I think we have a political wall." No doubt he was correct. Kudos for his honesty.

- A man from out of state who literally yelled at me on the phone over our differing political views and opinions. He proclaimed, "Clearly you do not have any grandchildren. If you did, you would believe and vote differently." I was shaking so badly after that conversation that I called a neighbor and asked if I could come over for a visit. I needed help to calm down. (P.S. I do have grandchildren and I did, in fact, vote with them in mind.)

- Another man who was shocked that differing political opinions could be a dealbreaker for me. His comment? "The election will be over shortly, and then none of this will matter." A short-sighted, ignorant perspective!

- The man who waited until I was three-quarters of the way to meet him at the ferry dock to say he'd missed the ferry because he had gotten the time wrong in his head. I called BS on that one. People who live on the islands here know the ferry schedule by heart.

Conclusion? You meet all kinds on the dating apps.

Yes, I would really like more consistent companionship. Yes, I want and need more hugs. Yes, it would be so nice to feel a warm presence in my home. And no, I am not willing to settle. My standards are high as are my hopes. I *know* my next soulmate is still out there somewhere.

JOURNALING DAY 17

Am I really all alone on this journey?

What's obvious and painful is that grief is everywhere. Even more so today in our tumultuous world, filled with economic uncertainty, political upheaval, and growing numbers of those infected/affected by the recent pandemic.

Grief may be invisible. People carry it around all the time—though to look at them, even talk to them, you'd never know. They don't know how to express it or they've been taught to just buckle up. They might not want to burden others. They have to be strong as others are counting on them. But in the end, if they've loved, they've lost.

Others are more willing to share their grief. Perhaps it is still so new, so raw, that they can't keep it stifled. Or they don't want to. There are those who realize the potential health impacts of swallowing up emotions and keeping them locked inside their bodies. Others just think they are being an adult.

The loss of my dear husband is still new, still raw. When, where, and how my grief expresses itself continues to surprise me. Certain lines in movies or TV shows bring tears to my eyes, as do ads about connecting with loved ones during times of isolation. Frustration can lead me to tears. Tasks I can't do, and those I don't understand. Tasks that Patrick did. Or shredding all those checks from a business I now need to close, accounts no longer active as our "community property" is no more. A jar of half-used face cream. Anything!

The flood gates can open while I'm listening to a song we both loved or lyrics that remind me of what we shared. Or when I hear the second movement of Beethoven's 7th Symphony.

In the words of Oscar Wilde, "You don't love someone for their looks, or their clothes, or their fancy car but because they sing a song only you can hear."

I will continue to soften into the pain, continue to breathe deeply. And yes, I will carry your song in my heart forever, my sweet love.

23
Enough About Me; What Did You Think About Me?

This encounter was a shock. It was another one of those men I thought could be a great match: a retired healthcare provider and photographer who loved to travel.

When I met Gary at his house, where he'd promised to cook me a lovely meal, he took me on a comprehensive tour, photograph by photograph, giving me a blow-by-blow description of each image, the place it was taken, and something about the subject matter. That was swiftly followed by a drive to a local gallery where several of Gary's photos were hung. Detailed information was shared about each of those pieces as well.

After the gallery tour, we returned to Gary's house, so he could start preparing dinner while I sat at the kitchen counter observing, my offer to help having been declined. He stopped to drink water to wash down the largest amount of vitamins, herbs, and contents of various other potions I've ever seen. They were, by the way, meticulously arranged and organized, occupying a substantial amount of space. Meanwhile, I enjoyed a glass of the wine I had brought.

The day was warm and sunny so when he asked me where I'd like to eat, I chose the patio. To reach the patio, we had to walk through the media room where there was an enormous TV screen, two easy chairs, and two TV trays. He stopped and said, "No, let's eat here." So we sat with our healthy, nicely prepared meal in front of the monster screen watching music videos. Frankly, I couldn't wait to leave. While Gary was tall, good-looking, in good shape, and intelligent, his idiosyncrasies were too unsettling for me.

In my fantasy, I've always thought being with someone in the medical field would be perfect. So the outcome of this encounter was very disappointing. As I left, I declined Gary's invitation to set up another date even though it was for some ping-pong competition, which I love.

JOURNALING DAY 18

What do I wish for myself?

What I hold for others, I hold for myself.

May we find:
...the stamina to persevere,
...the strength to endure,
...the courage to be real,
...the grace to forgive,

...the willingness to move forward,

...the permission to stumble,

...the commitment to self-care,

...the patience we deserve,

...the trust in our understanding,

...and faith in the process.

May we believe in ourselves and the power to heal.

24
Am I in India?

E ver had a day when you're glad you're wearing brown
pants? When you wonder if you should start carrying extra
underwear with you? Perhaps my body now revolts with even
more vigor when it doesn't like the situation I'm in. Maybe my
body knows more than my mind. That's probably a "yes."

They were nice enough men, certainly not threatening. And the
setting, in busy coffee shops, was quite public. However, the
timing and the circumstances were the worst.

Joshua was two months older than I. Definitely an aging hippie.
Long gray hair in a ponytail, scruffy beard, and a mustache.
Relatively sloppy clothing—ill-fitting jeans and an old T-shirt. He
was quite the Renaissance man with a laundry list of passions
and occupations, including licensed chiropractor, photographer,
film school graduate, furniture maker, landscaper, remodeler, and
fiction writer. We chatted over coffee for two hours, covering a
wide range of topics. Two things that definitely appealed to me: 1)
He was learning pickleball and enjoying it and 2) He reads quite
a bit. Any drawbacks besides the lack of chemistry? Two things
that didn't appeal to me: 1) He'd lost interest in traveling (not

necessarily a deal breaker) and 2) He constantly interrupted me when I was talking.

The morning was nice enough until my body revolted. It was *bad*. Thank goodness the only bathroom in the place was vacant. I literally excused myself mid-sentence and was gone for an "inappropriate" amount of time. When Joshua and I parted, we agreed we might see each other at pickleball.

George, another coffee date, reached out to me online asking, "Are you still looking for someone?" My response was, "I'm still open to meeting people." Somehow the way he phrased his question hit me the wrong way. Did it make me feel needy? Honestly, I admit to being sensitive about that. I've never thought of myself as needy. Is it needy to want a companion? Someone to snuggle, share laughter, stories, and despair about news events, and walk down random streets holding hands?

Awkwardly, my hour with George turned out to be a major shit show—literally. We made small talk, drank our coffee, and struggled through some conversation. He and I had very different interests. His are the environment, climate change, and protecting rivers and streams. He was passionate and wrote regularly about fishing and the fishing industry. I don't know much at all about fishing and it's not high on my list of curiosities.

After almost an hour, nature demanded an abrupt halt to the chatting. My body revolted in an irreparable, humiliating manner. I not only had to leave but also drive forty minutes back home before doubling back to watch my teammates play a tennis match. Over an hour wasted in travel alone.

P.S. I have traveled in India twice and am well acquainted with Delhi Belly. These experiences were equally embarrassing.

JOURNALING DAY 19

If I could tell Patrick all the ways I loved, admired, and respected him, what would I say?

To my partner of multiple lifetimes,

I remember your way with words, the written word, and your openness to communication. Your keen observational powers. Your magnetic eyes. Your tenderness. Your generosity. Your can-do attitude.

You were a hard worker, determined to do whatever was necessary to improve our life as a family. You encouraged each of us to do our best, to reach for a higher standard than we thought it was possible to achieve. Yes, sometimes you were demanding. But you were always a fierce protector of those you loved. And you believed in all of us.

Your creativity always touched my heart. Such a beautiful writer whose eloquent imagery always created crystal clear images. So expressive. Such a command of the written word. And your ability to see the light, to capture your subject's essence in your photography was unparalleled.

Your devotion to family. Your admiration of our children and devotion to their happiness. Your willingness to be the "bad cop" as they were growing up. Your fierce desire and hope that our grandchildren would grow up to love themselves and achieve their potential.

And how could I ever forget how helpful and supportive you were to me when my parents and brother died, and to Barbara when your brother Dennis was so ill and ultimately died? And to your other brother, Tim, through all of his adventures, ups, and downs. And the glee you felt when Tim finally moved to Portland and achieved some stability and happiness. What a trio you brothers were. Man, how you guys could laugh!

I loved our intellectual banter, your encouraging words, your kind and compassionate heart, and your warm and loyal friendship. A warm heart, a good soul, a gentle soul. What a warrior!

We shared a belief in the importance of lifelong learning. No problem or puzzle was beyond us. You were doggedly determined to figure out the difficult, to embrace the challenging. Traveling to other countries and navigating other cultures was definitely hard for you, but it certainly didn't stop your desire to know and understand more than met the eye. Your wicked intelligence and insight made you a valuable player on any team.

I admired your refusal to ignore problems, walk away, or look for the easiest solution. Not your style. You believed in justice and equity, graciously and generously contributing to causes that fed your conscience. It was hard to shred your 2020 presidential ballot . . . just sayin'.

So, my romantic Irishman, I will always remember your laugh, your smile, your caring spirit. Most of all, I will remember the feel of your arms around me, fully encompassing me. So much warmth, such strength, such love.

25
Nice Guys (Often) Finish Last

I do admit I like a bit of a bad boy. Not too much, just an edge, a bit of unpredictability. Patrick always used to bemoan the popular axiom about nice guys.

Willy, an older, rather esoteric guy, lived north of me. I might have been attracted to him back in the day. He described himself as a libertarian military brat in the past and now as a rational environmental agrarian. His professions and background were quite diverse. He says psycho-jargonists classify him as a "sigma male." According to AI, that term denotes "A man who is highly independent, self-reliant, and operates outside of traditional social hierarchies, often seen as a 'lone wolf' who doesn't conform to typical alpha behavior, preferring solitude and self-sufficiency over actively seeking dominance in a group." That sounds accurate. I do admit to being a bit curious about people, but I am always very careful not to lead anyone on. Our interaction was limited to written exchanges through the dating site. I wasn't sufficiently intrigued to pursue a face-to-face meeting.

Thomas was another man with whom I exchanged texts. He commented that he lives too far from Seattle but took the time to write anyway. He said, "After reading your profile, I just want to say that our world needs a lot more people like you." When I thanked him, he wrote back, "I just think that too many times things go unsaid that should not be." I was touched by his thoughtfulness and generosity.

JOURNALING DAY 20

What does my roadmap for moving forward look like?

As Lao Tzu, the ancient Chinese philosopher and writer, once said, "A good traveler has no fixed plans, and is not intent on arriving."

I have struggled with today's question all day. I am a true believer in not worrying about things that worry can't help (or change). I also spend no time or energy fantasizing about or imagining something that may or may not impact me in the future.

My best friend right now is my willingness to roll with the changes in the terrain, to not think too much about whatever is "up" for me. Experience it, explore it, feel it. No judgment. There is no such thing as a fixed plan in these circumstances. It is a journey of surprises—some good, some uncomfortable.

Every day, I am aware of the void, the absence of my most cherished friend. My heart will always grieve my loss. Some days, some moments, the grief is more intense than others. The deeper the love, the more profound the loss. Somehow I will learn to absorb my loss. While I trust the intensity of the pain will decrease over time, I know I will be changed forever.

The worst has happened. Patrick has died.

26
Beware of the Lazy and Unimaginative

Let's envision receiving messages from two men from two different cities. Each begins as follows:

"Hi Beautiful, thank you for allowing me the chance to get to know you. I believe that where there's a will, there's a way. I've been on this site for about a month now, looking for my soulmate, dream partner, lover, significant other, and life companion."

Each of these guys then describes what they do for a living, says they are a widower and that they have been single for X number of years. Then . . . "My daughter, who lives in the same city as you, is the reason I'm planning to move closer—so I can spend more time with my grandkids."

When I received the first message, I thought this man might be legit. I asked for more information about the name of the daughter's neighborhood and for a recent photo of the man, as none was included in his profile. I never received either, even after repeat requests.

Meanwhile, the opening message from the second man arrived. Given the identical verbiage, I quickly realized that both were a creation of AI, including the following request for my response to six questions.

1. What qualities do you appreciate in a man?

2. How many children do you have, and do they live with you?

3. What do you do for a living?

4. Can you tell me more about yourself?

5. What do you enjoy doing for fun and in your free time?

6. Have you met anyone on this site before? If so, how was your experience?

These questions raised another point of irritation: People don't read! I find this quite annoying. If you actually read someone's profile, someone who has taken the time to share information about themselves, some of these questions would be unnecessary. Responding to something you've read and asking a follow-up question helps you learn more about the person of interest, stimulating more meaningful conversation.

Anyway, receiving identical AI messages warranted a good laugh.

As an aside: I must say that I've been astounded at some of the photos men share of themselves. The ones where they are leaning against a wall as if it's the only thing holding them upright after a long night of drugs and booze. Then there are the bathroom shots, naked chest shots, or ones that show a room in complete disarray.

JOURNALING DAY 21

What memory still makes me laugh?

Hair. And lots of it. Good hair. He called himself black Irish. Dark hair. Radiant blue eyes. Patrick never made it to Ireland. The country was always on his wish list but it never happened—another abandoned, unfulfilled dream. We expected more time. We needed more time. We had so much life left to live.

But back to his hair. A headful of hair plus lots of facial hair. Beard, mustache . . . but not a lot of body hair. Worked for me.

Then one day, Patrick disappeared into the bathroom looking one way and emerged from it looking quite a different way. No more facial hair. "Why not try something new?" he said. "Right?"

"No, wrong!" I responded. He looked like his older brother, Dennis. Great guy, of course. But I had no interest in crawling into bed with Dennis.

So Patrick immediately reversed course. No more shaving. Let the hair grow. Meanwhile, for weeks, I had to close my eyes and listen to his voice to know that I was in bed with the man I loved. To know I was where I wanted to be, where I belonged.

Over the years, that head of hair grew thinner, more spotty. Enter the clippers. And the sexy shaved head. No more being mistaken for Michael Gross of *Family Ties* or Peter Frampton.

Bald man with facial hair = SEXY.

27

A Valiant Effort

On the fourth anniversary of Patrick's death, I decided to visit the exact spot where he had died. I wasn't ready to eliminate the Oregon coast from my list of getaways, so it was clear that sooner or later, I needed to relive the connection.

Climbing back on the horse, so to speak.

Standing on the exact spot in the parking lot of the inn where he had fallen, I read, "When Great Trees Fall" by Maya Angelou. Patrick was, indeed, a great tree, a strong man on whom I could always count.

The inn has a lovely garden that abuts the parking lot and the innkeepers were kind enough to not only me let me plant a bleeding heart but also to promise that they'd take good care of it. After planting it in Patrick's honor and memory, I read "Fear" by Kahlil Gibran. This was definitely a message for me to hear loud and clear. The last stanza reads as follows:

> The river needs to take the risk
> of entering the ocean

because only then will fear
disappear,
because that's where the river
will know
it's not about disappearing
into the ocean,
but of becoming the ocean.

Later that afternoon or perhaps the next day, several of us went to a local restaurant, sat outside, and enjoyed very large margaritas. While we sat there, my daughter, Michelle, surreptitiously stole my phone and wrote to a guy she had seen on my dating site. "You really need to meet my mom," she wrote. "I'm guessing you are someone who could keep up with her. She loves a comedy show and live music. I know she's a bit older than you, but honestly, she has more energy and spunk than any of my forty-something friends. Maybe you two could grab a drink and learn more."

Need I say it was all good for a laugh and I never heard from him?

But I gotta give my girl points for trying and for always supporting me.

JOURNALING DAY 22

How would Patrick try to help me calm down and believe that he is okay?

He might write to me, "Dear Babu . . . remember when your dad died? He came to me when I was meditating and said, 'If I'd known it was this beautiful, I would have left long ago.' He was so right.

"This is a land of peace, love, and softness. As I told Bryan, 'We move through the trees. The trees are like a network or conduit through which spirits can travel great distances.'

"Death is not lonely, Babu. Once you are here, it is like a reunion. People who came before me are now my guides, helping me along my new journey. Everything feels safe and warm and wrapped in love.

"This makes way more sense than planet Earth. You know I always felt like I was living on someone else's planet. I'm sure I was only there to find you again. But, it always felt foreign, unwelcoming.

"This realm is totally different. All those stories you read to me from the book *Final Gifts*, the book you said helped you feel better about or more accepting of the deaths of your father, mother, and brother—they were right. As you said, not that many people can be wrong. Or—not that many people can agree on something about which we have no proof. Something so magical and mystical.

"I think I'm lucky. I miss you desperately. And I miss Bryan, Michelle, Owen, and Kellen. But I am happy here. I am comfortable here. I feel safe and loved. There is no hate. There are no politics. This is human nature and pure consciousness at its best.

"I will hold a place for you. Someday we will be together again. Promise!"

28
Horrific Weather for This?!

We decided to meet halfway. Seemed only fair. The weather was truly atrocious. Not unusual for Seattle.

After ordering a drink and telling me how much he had in common with me, Steve brought out printed photos of his property and of each room of his house. I can only assume he was trying to invite me into his space. It didn't work. There was nothing inviting about him or the space.

While we had both spent a portion of our professional lives in education and shared a thirst for learning, there was a sense of desperation about Steve, of a life not lived. I felt like I could be swallowed up by a well-built beast—an unkempt beast, at that.

I've always been able to tell a lot about a person pretty quickly. I'm able to feel energy, especially connective energy—a trait that sometimes does not serve me well. In this case, my gut was accurate. I knew Steve was not a good match for me. There was no attraction whatsoever.

After we finished a light meal and spent plenty of time chatting, I said I needed to go. We left together and walked to his car to meet his dog. It was sad to see a large, filthy golden retriever who sorely needed grooming. I was sad for the dog. He didn't even look comfortable in his own skin.

The car was also filthy. Some people don't seem to understand that all these things say a lot about how they live and what's important to them.

Months later, Steve reached out to me again, clearly with no memory that we had met once before. Rather than just ignoring him, I reminded him of our previous meeting and politely declined the latest invitation.

Reaching out to the same person after months and months online is understandable. It's almost impossible to recall every interaction you've had. Clearly, some are more memorable than others.

JOURNALING DAY 23

How would I feel if Patrick was by my side right now?

If you were here with me now, I would feel safe and confident in your presence. You would listen to me and hold me while I cried. You wouldn't speak many words. You would just *be* with me and let me be. Under all the pain and aloneness, you would know that someday I will be okay.

You would share your confidence in me, your vision of me as strong and independent. You would encourage me to put that strong exterior aside and let out that soft, vulnerable side, express it in whatever way feels right to me.

You would take me out into the fresh air and encourage me to breathe deeply. We would walk together, mostly in silence.

You would talk to me calmly, saying it's okay to spend some time in a state called "lost," telling me I'll find my way out when I'm ready to move forward. And you'd remind me of my own words: "You can't push a river." This time, it's a river of tears.

And in your resonant voice, you'd say, "I am good. You will be too. So for now, just breathe, Babu. And trust."

29
Ulterior Motive

Ted was an interesting man I'd actually like to see again, though I think he was more curious about my father than about me. He plays several instruments and is still very involved with helping young people develop their musical skills.

I am reminded of how, for so many years, when I first met someone, they would ask, "Is Milton Katims your father?" Frankly, I was tired of the question. To me, he was my dad, a guy who put his pants on one leg at a time and took the garbage out.

So imagine my glee when my dad came home one day and told me that a random teenage boy had approached him outside the drug store and asked if he was *my* dad? I think I was fourteen at the time.

As for Ted, I found him engaging and very easy to talk to. He was definitely a good listener, very active, and seemingly interested in traveling. He was also handsome, in good shape, and invested in taking care of himself. I had a nice time with him at a symphony concert, an easy flow of conversation, but I walked away with no clue about how he felt about the evening. He is, by his own admission, "very chill" about relationships. Whether he is involved in one or not doesn't seem important to him. Ted is difficult to read and is definitely a slow burn.

Oh, the irony of it all. This time, I'd like more engagement; this time, *he's* saying, "Meh."

JOURNALING DAY 24

What messages am I receiving from Patrick?

When the sun is out, and I can see the mountains, I feel a glimmer of peace, even a hint of joy. Sunshine and visibility are not common at this time of year in Seattle.

Patrick has been in a number of my dreams lately, but I have not felt his presence in my waking moments.

In one dream, I was in a very large building. There was a hummingbird stuck inside; it fell and broke its beak. When the beak broke off, the bird grew much larger. I picked it up to take it outside, hoping it could survive. I put it in a tree where other animals might not be able to kill it. The bird flailed around. I'm not sure it lived.

I did my best to protect and save you, Patrick, but my efforts were insufficient. I couldn't control the uncontrollable.

In another dream, Bryan and I were playing tennis. One of his shots landed perfectly balanced on top of the net. It was not a tennis ball but a leaf, balanced perfectly between the two of us. A gentle, soft, delicate, but strong leaf. (There's always a nice balance of expression between power and gentleness.)

I wish Patrick would visit me in my waking life. I look forward to more signs of love and connection,

For now, my fleeting moments of joy are connected to sunshine, and spending time with my daughter, and soon with my son and his wife as well. We laugh and cry together, and it's all okay.

30
Blow-up Cars and Books

One night, I dreamed our family was still living in the home where we had raised our kids. I looked out the large living-room window to see four inflatable cars, each filled with people, pull so close to the house that they were almost touching the brick.

People emerged from the cars, knocked on the door, announced that several of them used to live in this house, and they wanted to look around. Without waiting for a response or an invitation, they pushed us aside and walked in. Half of them started poking around upstairs, while the other half went down below. It felt like an unadvertised "open house" as these strangers explored every nook and cranny, commenting on how things were the same or how they had changed.

My dream no doubt depicted how I felt after Patrick's death. Every part of my psyche, every part of my being, was being dissected and examined.

When all of these folks were out of sight, Patrick said he had something for me. He handed me a large, hardbound book, 8.5" x 11" in size and perhaps 1.5" thick. It was titled *Stories and Images of Patrick Steele*, curated by Wes Carter (I believe).

I panicked. *Does he know he is going to die? Does he know I am working on a book of his material right now?*

I had this dream on October 19, 2020, two months after Patrick's death. I was in the throes of working on a book to give to the kids for Christmas, a compilation of Patrick's writings and photography. A dear photographer friend of Patrick's was helping me compile this.

Without her help, I never would have made it. Together, we shared our tears, our incredulity, our love, and our loss.

The book, titled *The Heart of an Irishman*, is now a sweet reminder of my poetic English literature major husbandand is in the hands of the fifty people who most impacted Patrick's life.

Interestingly, many of us had been encouraging Patrick for years to publish his work. His constant refrain was an emphatic "No." No one would care, he argued, and no one would read it. He was such a gifted writer, great with words, great with imagery, a true romantic who could take three pages to describe something that I would do in one. He was the effusive one; I, the more pragmatic.

And here I am now, writing this book. Something I never imagined doing. Cathartic release and therapy come in many forms. I wish I had Patrick's poetic gift.

JOURNALING DAY 25

What would make me feel better today, other than the obvious?

I can't even respond to that. I truly don't know what to say. My tank feels empty. I long to find a source of hope. I long to be reassured that I will be okay. This road is not a steady climb in a "positive" direction. It is not linear. There are ups, downs, twists, and turns just like riding that horrible roller coaster. I thought I was through with that. I thought that was behind me. I thought I survived. And many people are not helping when they say, "What's going on? I thought you were beyond these feelings, this mood. You need to move on. It's time."

What do they know, really?

For now, I continue to trudge with exhausting effort.

31
The Relief of Distraction

In the winter of 2022, Linda, an old high school buddy, posted some photos of herself with a group of women, all in bathing suits, drinks in hand, and laughing while soaking up the sunshine in Bali. Seeing that photo took me out of myself, inviting me to think about what was next. I certainly understood that life was uncertain, there were no guarantees, and no one else was going to plan the next steps for me. I had to think and plan for myself.

In my note to Linda, I asked, "What does one have to do to join your tribe?" Her response was simple: "Just tell me you want to travel." I asked her to contact me when she returned to the States. She did, and we've never looked back.

Linda's goal is to visit a hundred countries before she dies. As I write this, I am on a flight from Doha, Qatar, to Mumbai, India. We are on a trip through Goa, Sri Lanka, Thailand, Malaysia, and Singapore. By the end of this adventure, Linda will have ninety-eight countries under her belt.

Traveling is a "rich" distraction. The opportunity to learn about other cultures, other people, and customs is an eye-opener. It's also a great lesson in perspective. I'm grateful that I have the resources and wherewithal to enjoy this gift. There is true beauty everywhere if you open your eyes and let the world in.

This is the third journey I've shared with Linda. Each has been unique, and each has taken me to lands I've never traveled. On our first adventure, we took a river cruise on the Lower Danube, visiting Romania, Bulgaria, and Serbia, and ending in Croatia. On our own, we saw Ljubljana in Slovenia, a city where I could live quite happily. At least I imagine I could. These cultures have so much more history than the United States. You can see it in the architecture, feel it in the walls of the buildings, and hear about it through the local stories.

On our second trip, we circumnavigated Ireland and had a brief stay in Oslo, followed by the "Norway in a Nutshell" trip to Bergen. Now that was stunning! The landscape and vistas were breathtaking.

Patrick's ancestors were from Ireland. Much to his disappointment, he never made it to his homeland. As I mentioned earlier, two trips were planned, and both had to be canceled. The best I can do with the dreams he is missing is to take his ashes with me wherever I go. He is becoming just as worldly as I, as I sprinkle a bit of him everywhere.

In trying to ease the pain of loss, we need to rediscover what feeds our soul, what puts a smile on our face, or shakes our body with laughter. Linda and I have been fortunate to meet people from all over the world whose sense of curiosity is just as cavernous as ours. We have shared many stories, an abundance of smiles, and some joyous laughter.

Traveling takes me to a new level of awareness. It opens my eyes and feeds my desire to learn.

But, given that I can't travel all the time, what else do I do to enrich my life? See Chapter 4 for a reminder. And, of course, I love to spend precious time with my kids and grandkids. What a joy to see how they all navigate their lives and the choices they make. They are certainly growing up in a very different world than I did. I can't say it's all comfortable, but again, we have no control over much of that.

Perhaps one positive outcome of Patrick's death is that I feel closer to both of my kids. We all share our loss and recognize how fleeting time is. Most likely, I am next on the conveyor belt, as Patrick would say, so I want to eke out as much time as possible with each of them. And after I'm gone, I pray—yes, I pray—that they will always love and support each other. They don't need to agree on everything; they don't even need to understand, but please, please let them accept, support, love, and be there for each other!

JOURNALING DAY 26

What does my "rearranged" life look like?

Life Rearranged

Patrick, architect of my heart

My soul connection

Navigation partner

Joy . . . love . . . hugs . . . life

The baby blues

Of lifetimes shared

No resisting

The power of love

Then shock, trauma, disbelief

Foreign terrain, unexplored chasm

Vapid . . . cold . . . alone

A starved heart

A shadow morphs

Omnipresent vacuum

Shape-shifter sidekick

Wailing transformation

The greediness of grief

Demanding

Debilitating

Numbing

Be with me

Sit in darkness

Allow, accept

Just love

Teach me

New rules, more patience

More forgiveness, less judgment

Self-care . . . self-love

Sorrow . . . not melancholy

Stubborn determination

I am injured

Not incapacitated

32

Honoring and Remembering My Love

Patrick died in the early months of COVID, so I went through excruciatingly lengthy alone time. It wasn't until nine months later, toward the end of May 2021, that we were able to have a memorial service, and even then, it had to be held outdoors.

While several aspects of this "celebration" (a term I wasn't yet ready to accept) were as expected—speakers, a comprehensive photo board, and a catered reception—there were a few unusual treats.

One of Patrick's favorite movies was *The Big Lebowski*. Referring to the movie, Patrick would say, "When I die, just put my ashes in a Folgers coffee can." Not only did we do that, but my daughter and I also put ashes in about forty smaller containers with homemade, professional-looking Folgers labels, inviting attendees to take some home, if they so wished. I suggested folks spread the ashes in their garden or someplace where they had perhaps walked with Patrick.

Friends and family knew something was up when they heard the theme song for a Universal Studios movie calling everyone together. It immediately elicited laughter and lightened the mood. Patrick would always crank up that theme song before a movie. He loved it.

The ceremony included live music performed by my son, his now-wife, and a wonderful guitarist friend of theirs.

During the reception that followed, we played a potpourri of songs, all of which had been suggested by Patrick's friends. Since so much time had passed between his death and the service, I asked folks to suggest a piece of music that made them think of Patrick. I ended up with over four hours of music on a playlist I call "Songs for Papa." Playing that is guaranteed to elicit any number of emotions and memories. I so appreciate having it.

A couple of years later, once our son Bryan and his wife Alixcia found their dream property, they created a heartfelt memorial to Patrick underneath a giant, protective tree. Buddha sits high on some stones with his beatific and calming smile. A small Folgers can containing Patrick's ashes sits next to him.

JOURNALING DAY 27

Rarely is there a traumatic event that doesn't carry some guilt and regret with it. While those feelings are not necessarily helpful, they're present. To ignore them can be destructive, leading to a delayed expression through emotional outbursts or physical symptoms, frequently

serious ones. It's important to ask myself: What regrets am I carrying?

IF ONLY

A split second. That's all it was. And my world changed, completely and forever. No discussion. No preparation. No "I love you." No goodbye.

A major earthquake rocked through my foundation, which came unhinged. My connection to reality severed. My compass smashed.

Dazed and confused. Sucked into the abyss where there is no bottom, no solid ground.

Last night, after climbing into that big, empty bed, I felt an intense pain in my solar plexus. The same spot as that on Patrick, where I had placed my hands, rhythmically performing CPR, all the while screaming for help. Screaming!

With last night's pain—more tears and then a journey into the land of regrets.

I wish I hadn't listened to him when he fervently insisted he would be fine.

I wish I had seen through his stubbornness.

I wish I had hugged him, put my head on his shoulder as he was asking me to do, instead of trying to connect to the internet to learn where we could find the closest medical help.

I wish I had spent more time next to his body in the ER after they had disconnected him from all that equipment.

I wish I had talked to him more as he lay on the table.

I wish I had been "present" instead of numb with shock and horror.

I wish I had sat with him at the mortuary before they cremated him.

I wish I had told him one last time how much I loved him.

I wish we'd never gone on that damn trip.

33

Subconscious Voices

Often, the subconscious tells us what our waking mind ignores, denies, or doesn't see. While we all dream, many people don't remember their dreams. Mine were vivid in the year or so following Patrick's death. Even so, I would often get out of bed during the night, wander to the dining room table in the dark, and make note of enough of my dream that I could reconstruct it in the morning.

In one dream, a female colleague and I were scheduled to shoot an important commercial for which we would be paid a handsome fee. My colleague unexpectedly got called out of town—permanently, never to return.

She left me high and dry, out in the cold with no resources to compensate for her departure. She left me alone with no warning. I flipped her off.

The meaning of this dream is clear: Patrick too had left me alone with no warning.

What's interesting is that I was not consciously aware of feeling anger toward Patrick. Rather, I felt uncertainty, fear, immense/intense pain, and isolation. It wasn't until I saw how quickly I was getting frustrated or angry with those around me that I knew I needed to seek outside counsel.

I warned the therapist that I was my own worst enemy, always the optimistic, perhaps unrealistic one, who believes she can handle anything on her own.

Doing this alone was not my best decision. Hearing myself process thoughts and feelings out loud, to someone else, helped me shed new light on where I was in my journey, how to take another step forward, how I judged myself, and how difficult it was to give myself permission to put expectations aside. My therapist helped me slow down and take the time to examine my patterns.

This need for more support was confirmed in yet another dream. I was setting up seven raffles for seven eye appointments. Lots of people were assisting.

While I initially feared that this dream meant I might be facing multiple healthcare appointments, I now believe it was more about accepting the help of others rather than believing I was capable of handling every project by myself. To see clearly, I needed help.

I was raised to be very independent. My parents traveled a lot, and I was left in the hands of caretakers. I grew to depend on myself and carried that practice into adulthood. Such independence is yet another double-edged sword.

JOURNALING DAY 28

What are some of the lessons I learned in our forty years together?

I see you in me. People always said we were so perfectly blended, our energy, our presence. With so many lifetimes together, we sensed the other, we reflected the other. There are some aspects of you that I have adopted, at least for now.

I'm learning how to amble, not be in a hurry. I'm softer now, not as intense, as you would say. I'm more patient but just as determined as ever. I'm working hard to draw on my inner strength, to stay connected to the here and now, and not get ahead of myself. I may be becoming more Irish—oy, just oy. Yeah, Jewish. I know. I can't totally squelch my heritage.

I'm seeing more darkness. I'm feeling more pessimistic. The weather is gray and wet, and I wonder why I'm here. You'd be lobbying for an escape to the sunshine.

On a more hopeful or positive note . . . you would be proud of me. I'm definitely more introspective than I used to be. I'm taking time to explore my feelings, working to attach a voice to my innermost thoughts. I am writing every day, something I admit often feels like homework. But like you, I am capturing my state of mind and heart and more frequently verbalizing it. It's a touchstone. A photograph with a painfully long exposure. And because I'm doing this, I will be able to revisit my words at a later time, helping me recognize the ways in which I've moved forward.

I am learning to look at my grief from so many perspectives. Frankly, it's exhausting. This grief is a heavy weight to carry.

In the midst of slogging through this swamp, I'm eternally grateful for the love, support, and compassion of our tribe. They are my crutches, my warm blanket, a source of pride and awe, a symbol of strength, and the reason to keep going.

I hope, in time, to be able to enjoy more belly laughs like you did. In time . . .

34
A Bit About Grief

There's often a fine line between honoring your grief and drowning in it. Between feeling the pain and allowing moments of joy to seep in. Between feeling numb and remembering to breathe.

It took time for me to remind myself that how I greeted each day was my choice. While we can't control much of what happens to us in life, we *can* control how we cope, the decisions we make, and whether to listen to our head or our heart.

Emerging from the constant pain and heaviness of grief takes time. It calls on us to be kind, gentle and patient . . . with ourselves. There is no timeline. There is no right or wrong. Each of us has our own process and must do our own work.

We're not a culture that deals well or gracefully with death. Most people don't talk about death until it's staring them in the face. When someone dies, many don't know what to say to the grieving survivors who are wracked with pain and sorrow. The truth, at least my truth, is that try as we might, we cannot know what someone else's pain feels like. It's impossible to imagine. It's impossible to understand. I know what it's like to lose the love of my life, but I don't know what it's like, for example, to lose a child. I can say it has to be horrific, but I don't *know* that level of pain.

My family never talked about death. Consequently, when my parents were in their waning months, I felt like I was flying by the seat of my pants. I was the ignorant executor who had to learn on the job. That's not the way to do things. It's hard to grieve and handle major decisions or to face the reality of loss and respond to consequential health, financial, and legal questions simultaneously.

And, in many ways, I was fortunate. I had resources I could rely on for help and support. Even so, I felt lost. I couldn't help but think about all those who have to navigate this complicated tangle on their own, those who don't speak English or have anyone to ask for advice.

Everyone's journey is different. And it's probably safe to say, they are all arduous. Every aspect of *my* journey has added to my life's lexicon. It's impossible to count all the lessons presented and learned, sometimes begrudgingly. Meeting people on dating sites continues to broaden my thoughts of "what if." Through the experience, I am better able to clarify my own hopes and desires. The men are traveling their own road. Finding the "right fit," one whose preferences, hopes, and dreams mesh with mine seems like a big ask. In the meantime, I'm open to possibility.

JOURNALING DAY 29

What was our magic all about?

Why We Worked

People put us on a pedestal. We didn't like it there. They thought we were the perfect couple. Neither of us knew what that really meant. But we did know that what those outside a relationship see or think they see is just that—only what they see, and therefore what they choose to believe. But drawing on an old analogy, they are only seeing the tip of the iceberg.

To this day, amid all my pain and visceral sense of loss, I still believe what you and I used to tell people when they asked us, "How do you do it? What's your secret?"

You and I cherished each other. And we prioritized each other's happiness above our own. We admitted that this only works if both people are committed to that principle.

I think we always had more belief in each other's gifts than we had in our own. We offered each other encouragement and gently nudged each other when we got stuck. We respected each other's minds, honored each other's hearts, and encouraged each other to grow, explore, and take risks. When necessary, we said, "Get your head out of your ass. You're being a jerk." We were so incredibly open and honest with each other.

The foundation of that iceberg was big, wide, strong, and solid. It took us years to build that together, but we were both stubborn and determined. We both knew we had found an unusual and rare jewel. As trite as it may sound, I was blessed to share forty years with you—at least in this lifetime. (The lyrics of the chorus in the song "Gandhi/Buddha" are still so fitting.)

I am burning a candle as I write this. To honor you and to remind me of the light that burns within me. Maybe by the power of suggestion, I'll seek and find more light to guide me on this journey. I love you, sweet Patrick—then, now, and forever.

And I pray that I'll find a shadow of this love story again.

35
The Dalai Lama's Visit

My mother died in January 2008. Two months later, in March 2008, the Dalai Lama and Desmond Tutu arrived in Seattle to participate in a week-long event titled "Seeds of Compassion." I volunteered to be on the communication committee, helping to ensure media access and accuracy and timely communication among presenters.

At the end of the conference, each volunteer committee was invited to have its photo taken with the Dalai Lama. I stood on the Dalai Lama's right side, the front of my left shoulder touching the back of his right shoulder. My left hand was virtually touching his rear end. *If I were my mother*, I thought to myself, *I'd pinch his butt.* He's such an imp that I'm guessing he would have laughed. In the end, however, I chickened out.

That night, I had an incredibly clear and distinct dream. The Dalai Lama came to me and said, "Your mother is all right. Don't worry, she is all right." And no, he and I had not shared a word about my mother.

My mother's death was one about which I had been feeling quite guilty. Lots of "shoulds": I should have done a better job taking care of her, making sure she had the best care possible. If I were a better daughter, I would have kept her in my home. I should have learned more about Alzheimer's. I should have been more understanding, less impatient.

The Dalai Lama's words and assurance were calming. They didn't eradicate my guilt, but they did help me reduce my negative self-talk.

JOURNALING DAY 30

What do I want for myself? What do I wish for, hope for? How can I now bless myself? What sort of meditation feels right?

May I give myself space and grace

To honor my heart

To acknowledge my truth

To be patient and breathe

To find courage and compassion

To be open to possibility

To find hope in tomorrow

To know I am worthy

36
Perspective, Five Years Later

The wall of self-protection surrounding me has softened. My eyes are no longer bloodshot and puffy from crying. I once again enjoy food and drink. I welcome a good laugh and some hearty competition on the tennis court. My heart no longer sits still in silence.

I'd be lying, though, to say that everything is rosy, fulfilling, and exciting. Life is different than it was. I am different. Some days, I don't recognize myself.

I desperately miss the man with whom I could celebrate and commiserate, bitch and banter. I miss those hugs. I miss the passion and the butterflies in my stomach. I miss knowing that someone always has my back.

But life goes on. The sun rises; the sun sets. While we may not see it, it's important to believe that it's there. It's important to be flexible, bend, stretch, and ultimately, get out of my comfort zone.

None of us knows the future with any degree of certainty. What I do know, however, is that without my favorite person by my side, the future remains more of a mystery than ever before. It's time to embrace it.

I have to dig deep to identify some positive things that have surfaced since Patrick's death. Some are totally frivolous, as I mentioned earlier, like eating popcorn and drinking wine and calling that "good enough" for dinner.

Other positives:

- I feel closer to my children.

- It's getting easier to ask for help. I can honestly say it's a sign of strength, not weakness.

- I've met some wonderful people who are also navigating painful changes. We all understand the rock 'n' roll ride, no explanations or excuses necessary.

- I'm exercising a wee bit more patience before I burst into tears over technology problems.

- I'm learning to live with disappointment. Frankly, I don't have much choice.

- I've traveled and met folks from all over the world.

- I'm learning about financial investments. It's scary, but I'm determined.

- I'm working hard to turn my attention from what is lost

to what is growing inside me, letting what is lost nourish what I'm becoming.

- I'm aware that I need to learn new ways to strengthen my core emotional and mental balance.

- I know I need to continue working on accepting disruptions, pain, and disequilibrium.

- I honor my vulnerability, my fluidity, and my resilience.

- I recognize that there will be lots more grieving in my life, loss of love, and loss of life. I hope I can always call on my strength and my support system to walk the path of pain with me.

- I'm doing a better job of focusing on mindfulness and gratitude.

Patrick and I got married on August 7, 1981. He was a Detroit boy who grew up in a blue-collar, Catholic family. His father was a labor consultant on the management side, his mother a homemaker who lived vicariously through glamour magazines and died from ovarian cancer at the age of forty-seven.

Although I was born in New York, my family moved to Seattle when I was in elementary school. My parents were both classical musicians who soon became important figures at the center of the Seattle arts and culture scene.

Patrick and I came from different worlds. He used to tease me by saying I grew up with a silver spoon. In comparison to his upbringing, maybe I did. The contrast didn't matter. I fell deeply in love with this man.

I first saw him walking up a steep hill in downtown Seattle after a normal workday. He was walking on the south side of the street, I on the north. He wore a dark suit and a trench coat with the belt buckled in the back, the front open to the breeze. This one-block journey became a ritual for two weeks as we each climbed the hill to meet our bus.

One morning, I was sitting with a work colleague and enjoying a cup of coffee in the restaurant on the street level of the building where I worked. Out of the corner of my eye, I saw a table with eight to ten people. The mystery man I saw every day was among them.

I saw him get up, coffee cup in hand, and head for a refill. As he came my way, I grabbed my colleague's arm and said, "Here goes." She had no clue what I was talking about.

As Patrick neared my side, I looked up and said, "Okay, stranger, so who are you?" He stopped. We introduced ourselves, discovered that we worked for the same company, and exchanged work numbers.

Our first lengthy conversation took place while we were eating lunch and people-watching on a park bench in Pioneer Square. As

I mentioned earlier, the connection was strong and swift. There was no denying the intense and passionate energy between us. So passionate it was that we married four months later, faster than either of us would have "planned," but I was already pregnant. Also unplanned but joyfully embraced.

The list of appropriate descriptors of Patrick is endless—creative, stellar communicator, romantic, intelligent, stubborn, hilarious, handsome, and dedicated to what soon became our family. People always loved seeing us together as we radiated joy.

We certainly had our challenges in the beginning. In fact, I vividly recall a disagreement that was so intense that Patrick said he was done—that he was walking out of there. He packed up the few things he had at my house and headed for the front door. When he opened the door and had one foot on the porch, I said, "I just have one question before you leave." He stopped, turned around, and looked at me when I quietly asked, "Is this the *way* you want this to end?" After mulling it over for only a few seconds, he walked back in, sat down on the couch, and we talked. He stayed.

Over time, we learned that we couldn't both be in the driver's seat. As Dan Fogelberg says, one has to navigate, and one has to steer. People can switch roles, which often works well depending on the nature of the task or issue. On the contrary, things don't go well if both people compete to do the same thing at the same time.

My parents were slow to warm up to Patrick. In their eyes, he wasn't good enough for me. They saw me with a doctor, a lawyer, a banker, and so on. But I was always attracted to creative, sensitive types—guys without fancy titles and healthy incomes. I doubt their feelings were unusual. Parents are typically quite protective of their daughters.

In the end, he became their hero, always willing to help with a task,

patiently guiding them in the use of basic technology, laughing at all my father's jokes, and serving as another pair of ears during their end-of-life decline.

PATRICK & PAMELA

37 YEARS IN LOVE

Patrick was "there" for each of us. Family was important to him. He basically saved me during what we called "The Crucible"—the decline and deaths of my father, mother, and brother. He coached our son's baseball team, happily drove to years of soccer matches, watched the girls' drill team with gleaming pride, and held my hand to calm me during our daughter's diving competitions.

A creative man filled with love, wisdom, and humor, he fed my every need for forty years. How rare a man. How lucky was I?!

Online Dating Through the Decades – Wisdom from Women in Their 30s through 70s

O ver the past year and a half of meeting men online, going out for coffee, wine, or a meal, feeling periodic attraction, but more often feeling frustration and disappointment, I found myself wondering if it's just me. Am I totally unrealistic in my hopes and expectations? Are my standards too high? Am I willing to compromise? Should I be? Am I just too old for this game? Should I give up?

All of these questions led me to reach out to others at different stages of life. To ask them about their experience. To find out if I'm alone. Boy, do the stories vary.

Representing the Thirty-Year-Olds:

Lauren

"I take my time, really evaluate men's pictures and what they write in their bio. If they don't write anything, I immediately move on, as that tells me they are not going to put in any effort. I look for kindness in their eyes. With my intuition and hardcore vetting, I have actually met some amazing men. I think we all would prefer to meet someone in person, and it could still happen, but it's hard to approach someone not knowing if they are single and/or being prepared to deal with possible rejection. Of course, someone could lie that they're single on the app. Dang cheaters."

Alisha

"In January 2025, after an eighteen-month hiatus from all dating sites, I did a complete reboot on my attitude. If I was going to get back into the online dating world, I needed to approach it differently.

"I stopped blaming outside factors, stopped blaming the apps, and stopped blaming the men. I changed my perspective and got clear on my intentions.

"I focused on myself, got healthy, and got involved in activities I really enjoy. Some of these activities actually put me in new environments where there was potential to meet a man with similar interests.

"I was ready for in-person dating events like speed dating and meet-up groups (for instance, Seattle groups such as Jigsaw and events such as Shuffle Dating).

"I spent time creating a more complete and honest profile in which I clearly outlined my dating intentions. I joined one app and had great conversations and dates. I worked hard on staying upbeat and optimistic and encouraged others around me to do so as well. It was important to surround myself with nurturing and positive energy.

"Starting in January 2025, I focused on finding a relationship that could lead to marriage. Knowing exactly what I wanted, being clear and concise about my goal was critically important.

"My belief? If you're going on the apps and are just willy-nilly, going with the flow, and don't know what you want, or if you are chaotic and unclear, your results will reflect just that. And it's not fair to those who are actually seeking a quality relationship.

"Another huge thing that I shifted was being deeply rooted in my healthy feminine. I knew I wanted and was seeking a man who was rooted in his healthy masculine.

"Of course, both energies are within us all, and it's a balance. When I am wearing my business-owner hat, I am in my masculine, controlling and leading. However, in a relationship, I want to be in my feminine, and my man to be in his masculine, leading and courting me.

"After two months of positive dating experiences, I downloaded another app. The very next day, I had my first date, just a casual meet-up for drinks to gauge the vibe. There was a great connection, and the conversation and level of honesty was mind-blowing. After our second date and more in-depth conversation, I thought, *Whoa, what's happening here!? And who is this man?!*

"After four dates, he asked me to be his girlfriend. I'm happy to report that I'm the happiest I've ever been. I am in love, and for the first time, I believe in my heart that this man is my future husband.

"I did this one differently. I promised myself that the next person I slept with was going to be my boyfriend. And that's exactly what happened. Protecting that part of myself and saving it for someone I truly care for and who cares for me and respects me feels more powerful than the sex-positive 'do whatever you want with whomever' attitude I used to have. I've officially been through the seasons of life, promiscuous and celibate, to get where I am today.

"It's been a heck of a journey through lots of potholes and ruts, but boy, have I learned along the way! See the smile on my face, and feel the love in my heart."

Representing the Forty-Year-Olds:

Michelle: Previously married, seeking a long-term relationship

"Dating apps have been a mixed bag for me. After my marriage of ten years ended, I turned to them with a sense of hope and curiosity, thinking they might be an efficient way to meet someone meaningful. Initially, I was very enthusiastic and put a lot of time and energy into the process. Over the past eight years, I've gone on more than fifty first dates, which has been exhausting in itself. Less than half of those ever led to a second date, which has left me feeling like meaningful connections are hard to come by. I've had three serious relationships from apps, each lasting around six months. Two of them ended poorly, which made me question my judgment and whether any of it is even worth the effort.

"To be fair, I've definitely had some fun over the years, but at this point, I feel fairly cynical about dating. I've put in the time and effort, but the outcomes have been disappointing more often than not. It's hard not to feel disillusioned when so many interactions feel shallow or transactional. I've come away from it all feeling generally disappointed in men and skeptical that anything real or lasting can come from swiping and small talk. I'm not sure what the path forward looks like, but I know I'm tired of investing in connections that don't seem to go anywhere.

"These days, the effort I put into dating, and my use of the apps, happens in fits and starts. I'm more focused on continuing to create meaning in my life with my dear friends and family, and I know that I don't need a man or a romantic relationship to complete me. That said, I haven't given up hope that 'my person' is out there somewhere. I guess old hopeful-romantic habits die hard."

Megan: Previously married, seeking a meaningful connection

"I've met some really interesting and fun people. I've also met some strange and, frankly, scary people. I believe a big reason people continue to try online dating is knowing that there's potential to meet someone great. Unfortunately, the reality is that online dating companies are businesses, and they exist to make money. As the years go by, the process becomes more 'gamified,' and these companies prey on people's emotions by using a nickel-and-dime tactic, charging them for every 'opportunity' to increase their odds of matching with someone. Despite the questionable ethics of these business practices, people still turn to online dating because we conduct a lot of our lives online now, and it's the most convenient way to access other individuals who are looking for partnership. It's an inconvenient truth.

"I've been using online dating platforms for over ten years. What I have learned is this process should be supplemental to developing yourself as a friend, parent, colleague, and overall human being. Don't wait for some kind of magical moment—brought to you by a dating app—to change your life, because that's not reality. You might get lucky and find someone great, but you might not, and it's not worth wasting quality time hoping that will happen."

Representing the Fifty-Year-Olds:

Elaine: Never married, seeking a long-term partner

"Online dating is a necessity in modern life, and especially so as you get older and there are fewer opportunities to meet even fewer single men. I don't find it enjoyable or even very effective, but I have accepted that there aren't other good options if you want to increase your odds of meeting a long-term partner. On top of that, many men who are single in their fifties are divorcing or recently divorced, and they are not in the right mindset for a healthy relationship with someone their own age.

"In the early 2000s, online dating was more fun and productive. Fewer people were doing it back then, and those people were more intentional and open. It was a little taboo back then, and you kept how you met your boyfriend to yourself. At that time, I was still meeting people through work and both channels were equally useful for meeting and dating.

"In the 2010s, things changed. The men online were flaky and judgmental—scrutinizing everything they saw and didn't see in your profile and drawing unfounded conclusions about suitability and interest. In my experience, men wanted to carry on with long messaging relationships that often did not lead to an in-person meeting, because they were too busy, distracted, or uninterested. Just like on any other social media, people are more willing to be assholes or unreliable when they know they won't just run into you or get asked about it by mutual friends. You're a stranger with no connection to their real-life friends. Because I was so disappointed with online dating, I tried another pathway and joined a marathon fundraiser team. I met a married man who pretended to be single and a bunch of women more than fifteen years older than I. It wasn't fruitful.

"In the 2020s, I have a more pragmatic approach. I won't chat back and forth for too long without commitment for an in-person meeting. I'm willing to meet people a second time even if there wasn't a great connection the first time around. I don't respond or reach out to people who are long-distance or above or below five years of my age.

"But this story has a happy ending. Over a year ago, I met a wonderful man who I nearly passed over because his profile was sparse and he looked like an outlaw with his 'COVID beard' picture. After four dates (slow burn), I knew he was the man for me. It turns out he's exactly the opposite of how his profile came across. He is funny, highly educated, curious, informed, kind, a great lover, and very stable and responsible. Life is full of twists and turns, and I don't actually know if our circumstances will align long term, but for now, I am in love and happy to be offline."

Kat

"My experience with online dating in my fifties has not been very successful.

"First off, understand that I am very sex-positive. It's important I know immediately if I am sexually compatible with someone. I do not want to waste my time on someone with whom I can't have epic sex. Life is short. Go for what you want.

"I've been on several dating websites. My overall assessment is that I'm not attracted to men around my age, and surprisingly, the ones that are slightly younger are already having penis problems. Let me count the ways, lol!

"My first experience was with a very sweet man who is still a dear friend. We had a great time together, but he had Peyronie disease, in which fibrous scar tissue inside the penis causes curved, painful erections. It was impossible for me to have an orgasm the way I normally do. His penis would not reach the spot. Believe me, I tried! As sex is very important to me, I had to tell him that it was not going to work. Luckily, he understood and was okay with this. We now see each other a few times a month as friends.

"Some of my other adventures?

1) A man with an immediate ejaculation upon entry, mixed with weed addiction. One and done.

2) A gorgeous man with a terrible personality and the worst ED I have ever experienced! He didn't even recognize that he had a problem. We tried again on another day but got the same result.

3) A sexy, swarthy man that I tried dating for a few months. He also had ED and was painfully aware of it but unwilling to do anything

about it. His penis wasn't limp but would not get fully hard. He was able to enter me but not to the point where it was enjoyable. So frustrating! I suggested pills several times. He just swept it under the rug.

"Not all of my experiences were bad, sexually, but they did help me better define what I am looking for in a relationship. I tried to adjust my age range to younger men out of sheer sexual frustration. I found out quickly that if you want to be a cougar, that won't be a problem! My message board lit up!

"I think it is trendy to have a few cougar notches on the bedpost at this point in time. I tried to go out with a younger man, but the whole time the voice in my head was shouting, *You're old enough to be his mom!*

"The following story represents quite a quandary. This guy was thirty-eight and had the physique of a competitive fitness athlete. The most beautiful man I had seen in a long time. He was upfront about his non-monogamous lifestyle. That was fine with me. I just wanted to experience what it would be like to have sex with someone so physically perfect, and he was! I have never done this, but I had him come to my house before I even met him in person. It was like a porn movie. He walked in, and we immediately started kissing passionately. Then, it was straight to my bedroom where we proceeded to have incredible sex. Perfect penis, rock hard! Lasted a perfect amount of time, after which we lay there talking for a while before going at it again. More technically amazing sex. Had there been an emotional connection, I would have called it epic.

"That was the only time we had sex, but we stayed friends, and he became my personal trainer for a three-month intensive online fitness program. I'm not sure about this, but maybe this was a strategy to gain clients? He asked to hook up with me again, but I turned him down. This was fun and satisfying but, ultimately, I want an emotional connection and a partner in life.

"Lastly, I dated a man my own age whom I met through a friend. This one is a head-scratcher. While we had an emotional connection, I wasn't sure about his station in life—his career, home life, etc., so I told him I wasn't looking for a serious relationship. He seemed to have ED at first, but the second time we hung out, I asked him to take a pill, and he had no problem. *Epic* sex! After that, he no longer needed a pill. Perhaps he just needed a jumpstart.

"We dated each other for five weeks when I started to realize that he was falling in love with me. I reminded him that I wasn't looking for a serious relationship and asked him how he would feel if I was dating other people. He got upset and basically acted like I hadn't asked that. It all ended badly.

"After that experience, I decided to give my ex another shot. Bad idea. They are exes for a reason!

"I hope this rant does not deter anyone from trying to find love. I am now in an amazing relationship with someone I met at a friend's party. Definitely an easier way to meet someone than on the dating sites. He told me that before me he had to take pills to perform. I would not have guessed that, as we have epic sex without pills. At least I know he will be open to it when needed.

"I believe that ED is not something to be ashamed of, and it happens to most men when hormones change as we age.

"The moral of my story is: Don't settle. *And* gentlemen, take the pills!"

Representing the Sixty-Year-Olds:

Danielle

"Like many others, I will give online dating a mixed review. Early on, I met two mentally unwell men who slipped through my online "vetting" process, a process I thought I had nailed. But no harm, no foul for the most part . . .

"More importantly, I met two men with whom I have remained friends! After our (pretty darn good) adventure-filled summer relationship, and at times steamy romance, completed its course, the first one ended up marrying someone else and ultimately divorcing. I'm happy to say that we ended up much better platonic friends than lovers—and still are to this day! We both enjoy sharing deep conversations.

"The second man reminded me a little too much of my ex-husband . . . yep, the one who had an issue with alcohol! However, as time passed and I got to know him better, I realized with a dose of regret that I had 'let a really good one get away.' He eventually married another woman and moved out of the country. For a while, we continued our friendship, but unfortunately, that's no longer the case. We've lost touch.

"I have no great successes to regale you with. I'm currently taking a break waiting for the stars to align or realign."

Annie

When I initially ventured into online dating, I was in my late 40s. Back then, my wrinkles were fewer, and so were the number of online dating sites. At the time, the two top sites were Match.com and eHarmony. I chose the latter. They required answers to more than forty questions. I figured that any man who would go through all of them was more serious about finding the right person. I sifted through onslaughts of inquiries. More than seven hundred in total. Out of that, I responded to a handful, dated three men over the course of a year, and fully enjoyed the experience.

"Fast-forward fifteen years. I'm in my early sixties. The number of online dating sites has exploded, but the number of inquiring men has not. I'm not sure how much of that is related to the fact that there are so many different options for connecting, or maybe I was just kidding myself.

"I was back on eHarmony, searching for authenticity, which also meant that I needed to project authenticity. But how much? Any close-up photos would show the wrinkles, grey hair, and shorter stature. Any professional photos might come across as too career-oriented for anyone who is retired. Any photos with family might scare them away.

"So I kept it simple and reminded myself that it just takes one. The irony? He showed up in the first three days. A man I had met professionally thirteen years earlier.

"We started with emails. Then three Zoom conversations. And as soon as we met in person, we both believed, 'This is it.' Fate must have brought us together.

"That relationship lasted two years. So clearly, it wasn't 'it.' Even though it didn't last, I will always hold him in my heart.

"Will I get back online and try it again? Perhaps in time. Next time, I'll be a little more judicious. I won't start out looking for 'the one' online and instead just have fun with it."

Representing the Seventy-Year-Olds:

Deb

As of April, 2024, after four years of living with my husband's cancer diagnosis, I find myself in a new stage of life: seventy and widowed. I miss connection. I miss touch. I miss friendship.

Six months after my husband died, I was surprised to experience a dynamic attraction to another man. Our feelings for each other led to warm embraces. That's it. Nothing more. But those embraces showed me that I was still capable of feelings. We flirted intensely on and off for several months. After time, however, it was apparent that the more than ten year age difference (me being older), was not going to work. We decided to go our separate ways.

Since I was curious about online dating, I joined a couple of sites. I met two men, each in the seventies, twice for coffee. Both seemed like a match but in person, that was not the case. I am active, pretty fit and neither held my interest, even through coffee.

I exchanged messages with a couple of others, only to eventually be ghosted. In addition, I was scammed twice, though it took me some time to realize it was happening. I think I suspected it from the beginning, but I didn't want that to be the case.

Then there was the sixty-six year old who said he "wanted someone younger". My reply was "me too"!

Recently, I deleted all dating apps. I have found solace in friendship with two very nice men (widows older than me) and plan to continue our friendship.

I am in my second year of being a widow. For now, I am content and at peace with my life as it is. I am active with my family, my grandsons, pickleball, kayaking, hiking and dancing...to name a few. Life goes on. Life is good. That's my choice.

All that - and yes - I continue to miss warm embraces.

Pamela, your author

"I believe that my age is an enormous factor in the world of online dating. At least, that's the story I tell myself. It's a big number. However, I'm not your typical seventy-eight-year-old. My photos tell part of that story. My activity level and energy tell another part. A critical part.

"I have a number of widowed friends, none of whom are dating and/or willing to enter the world of online dating. They're living through me, vicariously. At least I can keep them entertained.

"You've no doubt surmised that my experience with online dating has been less than satisfying thus far. I know it's a business, and I know I don't have a lot of alternatives if I want to continue meeting people. Whenever my subscription nears expiration, I tell myself that I'm not going to renew it. And then I do. I continue to cling to hope.

"A bigger or better hope and dream is that a friend will excitedly come forward to introduce me to someone they know. The initial vetting or research will have been done. This would be a friend who knows both of us and can predict a good connection. At least, that would be a stronger start than the blind one online.

"There's also the option of trying different sites. I've done a bit of that and can't say that the results have been markedly different. Maybe it's like shopping at Costco. If you're there and see something enticing, buy it, as it won't be there the next time you're shopping. Men will come and go on different sites, as will I. Matching up in a meaningful way is a crapshoot and a time suck.

"I try to see the humor in all of it, as well. And what can I say—it's given me some good fodder for this book.

"My hunger, my sense of longing stays with me. *Nights of Hunger*—originally named for 'The Northerner'—is still an apt descriptor."

Epilogue
My Hope for You, My Readers

Thank you for going on this journey with me. Hopefully, you have laughed, perhaps learned a few things, and have recognized, along the way, that none of us is alone.

I hope you now have better tools to . . .

- Recognize that you can survive tragedy.

- Be patient with yourself.

- Acknowledge that grieving timelines do not exist.

- Give yourself the grace and compassion that you would offer a dear friend.

- Believe that joy and hope will once again be part of your future.

- Be open to new experiences.

- Be proud of the courage it takes to get through each day.

- Be amazed at your own strength and determination.

- Meet new people and be open to finding love in your life once again.

- Be better prepared to support a grieving friend or family member.

I honor each of you, wherever you are on your path, and encourage you to be the best you can be. To be compassionate, loving, trustworthy, and ever-evolving.

Acknowledgments

With sincere appreciation:

- To my supporters, whose open hearts and accepting shoulders continue to give me strength.

- To my "kids," Michelle and Bryan, for your vulnerability, openness, honesty, and willingness to walk this road by my side. On a more 'academic note,' thank you for your ongoing feedback and edits. I hope you write your own book someday. You're both quite gifted!

- To Michelle for all your help with technology. I'd have no hair by now had I been left to my own devices.

- To all my editors for your thoughtful, constructive feedback.

- And to all the men who have unknowingly expanded my world.

May the stars continue to light the path and the sun warm our backs.

Made in the USA
Monee, IL
02 July 2025

20219795R00100